Stimmt!

AQA GCSE German
Foundation
Vocabulary Book

Pearson

Published by Pearson Education Limited, 80 Strand, London, WC2R 0RL
www.pearsonschoolsandfecolleges.co.uk
Text © Pearson Education Limited 2017
Editorial management by Gwladys Rushworth for Haremi
Edited by Anne Urbschat
Typeset by York Publishing Solutions Pvt. Ltd.
Cover image: Getty Images: PhotoDisc / Kathrin Ziegler
Cover © Pearson Education Limited 2017

Written by Melissa Weir

First published 2017
10 9 8 7 6 5 4 3

British Library Cataloguing in Publication Data
A catalogue record for this book is available from the British Library.
ISBN 978 1 292 17254 5

Copyright notice
All rights reserved. No part of this publication may be reproduced in any form or by any means (including photocopying or storing it in any medium by electronic means and whether or not transiently or incidentally to some other use of this publication) without the written permission of the copyright owner, except in accordance with the provisions of the Copyright, Design and Patents Act 1988 or under the terms of a license issued by the Copyright Licensing Agency, Barnard's Inn, 86 Fetter Lane, London EC4A 1EN (www.cla.co.uk). Applications for the copyright owner's written permission should be addressed to the publisher.

Printed in the UK by Ashford Colour Press

Inhalt

High-frequency words **4**

Kapitel 1
Words I should know for speaking and writing activities **13**
Extra words I should know for reading and listening activities **15**

Kapitel 2
Words I should know for speaking and writing activities **16**
Extra words I should know for reading and listening activities **18**

Kapitel 3
Words I should know for speaking and writing activities **19**
Extra words I should know for reading and listening activities **22**

Kapitel 4
Words I should know for speaking and writing activities **23**
Extra words I should know for reading and listening activities **26**

Kapitel 5
Words I should know for speaking and writing activities **27**
Extra words I should know for reading and listening activities **30**

Kapitel 6
Words I should know for speaking and writing activities **31**
Extra words I should know for reading and listening activities **34**

Kapitel 7
Words I should know for speaking and writing activities **35**
Extra words I should know for reading and listening activities **37**

Kapitel 8
Words I should know for speaking and writing activities **38**
Extra words I should know for reading and listening activities **41**

High-frequency words

Common verbs

abfahren	to depart
ankommen	to arrive
sich beeilen	to hurry
besuchen	to visit
bleiben	to stay
eintreten	to enter
fahren	to drive
fallen	to fall
hineingehen	to enter
sich hinsetzen	to sit down
kommen	to come
laufen	to walk, to run
einen Spaziergang machen	to go for a walk
spazieren	to walk
springen	to jump
steigen	to climb, to get on
verlassen	to leave (a place)
vorbeigehen	to pass by
zurückfahren	to return
zurückgehen	to return
zurückkehren	to return
zurückkommen	to come back
halten	to stop, to hold
holen	to fetch
kleben	to stick, to glue
klopfen	to knock
laden	to load, to charge
öffnen	to open
schlagen	to knock, to hit
schließen	to shut
stecken	to put
stellen	to put
tragen	to wear, to carry
zumachen	to close, to shut
zurückstellen	to put back

Had a look ☐ **Nearly there** ☐ **Nailed it** ☐

begleiten	to accompany
bringen	to bring, to take
fliehen	to escape
folgen	to follow
führen	to lead
landen	to land
fallen lassen	to drop
leben	to live (to be alive)
nehmen	to take
parken	to park
schlafen	to sleep
sterben	to die
stoppen	to stop
warten auf	to wait for
wohnen	to live (in a)
lassen	to leave
legen	to lay
liegen	to lie
sitzen	to sit
werfen	to throw
sich amüsieren	to enjoy oneself
arbeiten	to work
ausleihen	to lend
einladen	to invite
einschlafen	to fall asleep
essen	to eat
fressen	to eat (animal)
fernsehen	to watch television
forschen	to research
klettern	to climb
sich kümmern um	to look after
sich langweilen	to be bored
lernen	to learn
lesen	to read
schenken	to give (presents)
studieren	to study (at university)
im Internet surfen	to surf the internet
(sich) treffen	to meet
trinken	to drink
verbringen	to spend (time)

Had a look ☐ **Nearly there** ☐ **Nailed it** ☐

sich ärgern	to be annoyed
bedauern	to regret
sich erinnern (an)	to remember
fühlen	to feel
gehören	to belong
helfen	to help
lächeln	to smile
lachen	to laugh
leid tun	to be sorry
lieben	to love
lügen	to tell a lie
meinen	to think, to say
(sich) streiten	to argue
vergeben	to forgive
vergessen	to forget
vermissen	to miss

Had a look ☐ **Nearly there** ☐ **Nailed it** ☐

aufmachen	to open
sich befinden	to be located
begegnen	to meet
berühren	to touch
drücken	to push

High-frequency words

verpassen	to miss	anfangen	to begin
versprechen	to promise	aufhören	to stop
verzeihen	to forgive	beenden	to end
weinen	to cry	beginnen	to begin
wissen	to know	dauern	to last
wünschen	to wish	enden	to finish, to end
		erreichen	to reach

Had a look ☐ **Nearly there** ☐ **Nailed it** ☐

		geschehen	to happen
		gewinnen	to win
anrufen	to phone	nachsehen	to check
antworten	to answer	notieren	to note
beantworten	to answer	organisieren	to organise
beschreiben	to describe	passieren	to happen
besprechen	to discuss	planen	to plan
sich bewerben um	to apply for	produzieren	to produce
denken	to think	scheitern	to fail
diskutieren	to discuss	schiefgehen	to go wrong
erklären	to explain	verbessern	to improve
erzählen	to tell	verlieren	to lose
fragen	to ask	versuchen	to try
informieren	to inform	vorstellen	to introduce
mitteilen	to inform		

Had a look ☐ **Nearly there** ☐ **Nailed it** ☐

plaudern	to chat		
reden	to talk		
sagen	to say	bedienen	to serve
schreiben	to write	befehlen	to order (command)
sprechen	to speak	benutzen	to use
eine Frage stellen	to ask a question	beraten	to advise
telefonieren (mit)	to phone	bestellen	to order (food)
tippen	to type	bitten um	to ask for
unterschreiben	to sign	danken	to thank
wiederholen	to repeat	empfehlen	to recommend
zuhören	to listen	füllen	to fill

Had a look ☐ **Nearly there** ☐ **Nailed it** ☐

		geben	to give
		gelingen	to succeed
annehmen	to accept	raten	to advise
bekommen	to receive	reparieren	to repair
beschließen	to decide	reservieren	to reserve
bevorzugen	to prefer	retten	to save, to rescue
brauchen	to need	schicken	to send
sich entscheiden	to decide	wechseln	to change

Had a look ☐ **Nearly there** ☐ **Nailed it** ☐

erhalten	to receive		
erlauben	to allow		
erwarten	to expect	finden	to find
fehlen	to be missing	glauben	to believe, to think
sich freuen auf	to look forward to	haben	to have
gefallen	to please	heißen	to be called
gern haben	to like	hoffen	to hope
hassen	to hate	hören	to hear
sich interessieren für	to be interested in	kennen	to know (be familiar with)
verhindern	to prevent	nennen	to name
vermeiden	to avoid	schauen	to look
vorhaben	to intend	scheinen	to seem, to shine
werden	to become	sehen	to see
		verstehen	to understand
		wählen	to choose, to dial

Had a look ☐ **Nearly there** ☐ **Nailed it** ☐

5

High-frequency words

zeigen	to show	geduldig	patient
dürfen	to be allowed to	gesund	healthy
können	to be able to	glücklich	happy
mögen	to like	gut gelaunt	in a good mood
müssen	to have to	komisch	funny, comical
sollen	to be supposed to	lustig	funny
wollen	to want	nett	kind, nice
zusehen	to look, to watch	reif	mature, ripe

Had a look ☐ **Nearly there** ☐ **Nailed it** ☐

reizend	charming
schnell	fast, quick
stark	strong
stolz	proud
verantwortlich	responsible
zufrieden	satisfied

ausgeben	to spend (money)
einkaufen	to shop
einschalten	to light, to turn on
kaufen	to buy
klicken	to click
klingeln	to ring
kosten	to cost
leihen	to borrow, to hire
mieten	to rent, to hire
schneien	to snow
schweigen	to be silent
stehlen	to steal
verdienen	to earn
verkaufen	to sell
zahlen	to pay
zählen	to count

Had a look ☐ **Nearly there** ☐ **Nailed it** ☐

groß	big, tall
klein	little, small
lang	long
kurz	short
hoch	high
niedrig	low
breit	broad
schmal	slim, narrow
dicht	dense
eng	narrow, tight
dünn	thin
rund	round
steil	steep
nah	near
weit	far
voll	full
leer	empty
erst–	first
letzt–	last
nächst–	next

Had a look ☐ **Nearly there** ☐ **Nailed it** ☐

Common adjectives

ärgerlich	annoying
böse	angry
dumm	stupid
eilig	in a hurry
ermüdend	tiring
ernst	serious
erschöpft	exhausted
faul	lazy
launisch	moody
laut	loud, noisy
müde	tired
schüchtern	shy
schwach	weak
schwer	heavy, serious
streng	strict
traurig	sad
zornig	angry

alt	old
jung	young
jünger	younger
dick	fat
schlank	slim
hübsch	pretty
schön	beautiful
hässlich	ugly
krank	ill
reich	rich
satt	full

Had a look ☐ **Nearly there** ☐ **Nailed it** ☐

Had a look ☐ **Nearly there** ☐ **Nailed it** ☐

artig	well-behaved
brav	well-behaved
beschäftigt	busy
dankbar	grateful
dynamisch	dynamic
fleißig	hard-working

gut	good
ausgezeichnet	excellent
fantastisch	fantastic

High-frequency words

großartig	magnificent
klasse	sensational
perfekt	perfect
prima	marvellous
toll	great
wunderbar	wonderful
Lieblings-	favourite
aufregend	exciting
spannend	exciting, tense
ekelhaft	disgusting
enttäuscht	disappointed
langweilig	boring
schlecht	bad
schrecklich	awful, terrible

Had a look ☐ **Nearly there** ☐ **Nailed it** ☐

bequem	comfortable
dreckig	dirty
flexibel	flexible
gebrochen	broken
gefährlich	dangerous
geöffnet	open
geschlossen	closed
heiß	hot
kaputt	broken
kostenlos	free (of charge)
neu	new
nötig	necessary
notwendig	necessary
offen	open
sauber	clean
schmutzig	dirty
teuer	expensive
umweltfeindlich	environmentally damaging
umweltfreundlich	environmentally friendly
weich	soft
zerbrochen	broken

Had a look ☐ **Nearly there** ☐ **Nailed it** ☐

allgemein	general
bestimmt	definite
echt	real(ly)
wahr	true
richtig	correct, right
falsch	false
aktuell	current
ehemalig	old, former
genau	exact
gleich	same
gültig	valid
klar	clear
möglich	possible
nützlich	useful
typisch	typical

unterschiedlich	variable
wertvoll	valuable
wichtig	important
wirklich	real(ly)
zahlreich	numerous

Had a look ☐ **Nearly there** ☐ **Nailed it** ☐

alle	all
eigen	own
ander–	other
einzig	only
allein	alone
zusammen	together
leise	quiet
lautlos	soundless, silent
friedlich	peaceful
ruhig	calm
frei	free, vacant
bereit	ready
fertig	ready
leicht	easy, light
schwierig	difficult
schwer	hard, heavy, difficult
erstaunlich	astonishing
unglaublich	unbelievable
unvorstellbar	unimaginable
erfreut	pleased
erstaunt	astonished
überrascht	surprised

Had a look ☐ **Nearly there** ☐ **Nailed it** ☐

Common adverbs

oben	above, upstairs
unten	below, downstairs
vorwärts	forwards
rückwärts	backwards
hier	here
da	there
dort	there
da drüben	over there
irgendwo	somewhere
draußen	outside
mitten (in / auf / an / …)	in the middle of
unterwegs	en route, on the way
immer	always
oft	often
regelmäßig	regularly
manchmal	sometimes
kaum	barely, hardly
nie	never
neulich	recently
sofort	immediately, straight away

Had a look ☐ **Nearly there** ☐ **Nailed it** ☐

High-frequency words

besonders	*especially*
sehr	*very*
wirklich	*really*
ziemlich	*rather, quite*
zu	*too*
immer noch	*still*
fast	*almost*
genug	*enough*
jedoch	*however*
leider	*unfortunately*
vielleicht	*perhaps*
wahrscheinlich	*probably*
besser	*better*
gern	*willingly*
lieber	*rather (preferably)*
mehr	*more*
nur	*only*
schon	*already*
langsam	*slowly*
schnell	*quickly*

Had a look ☐ **Nearly there** ☐ **Nailed it** ☐

Prepositions

bis	*until*
durch	*through*
entlang	*along*
für	*for*
gegen	*against*
ohne	*without*
um	*around*
wider	*against*

Had a look ☐ **Nearly there** ☐ **Nailed it** ☐

aus	*out of*
außer	*except*
bei	*at, with, next to*
gegenüber	*opposite*
mit	*with*
nach	*after*
seit	*since*
von	*from*
zu	*to*
hin zu	*towards*

Had a look ☐ **Nearly there** ☐ **Nailed it** ☐

an	*at*
auf	*on*
hinter	*behind*
in	*in, into*
neben	*next to*
über	*above, over*
unter	*beneath, under*
vor	*in front of*
zwischen	*between*

Had a look ☐ **Nearly there** ☐ **Nailed it** ☐

statt	*instead of*
trotz	*despite*
während	*during*
wegen	*because of*

Had a look ☐ **Nearly there** ☐ **Nailed it** ☐

Colours

die Farbe	*colour*
blau	*blue*
braun	*brown*
dunkel	*dark*
gelb	*yellow*
grau	*grey*
grün	*green*
hell	*light*
lila	*violet*
rosa	*pink*
rot	*red*
schwarz	*black*
weiß	*white*

Had a look ☐ **Nearly there** ☐ **Nailed it** ☐

Numbers

eins	*one (1)*
zwei	*two (2)*
drei	*three (3)*
vier	*four (4)*
fünf	*five (5)*
sechs	*six (6)*
sieben	*seven (7)*
acht	*eight (8)*
neun	*nine (9)*
zehn	*ten (10)*
elf	*eleven (11)*
zwölf	*twelve (12)*
dreizehn	*thirteen (13)*
vierzehn	*fourteen (14)*
fünfzehn	*fifteen (15)*
sechzehn	*sixteen (16)*
siebzehn	*seventeen (17)*
achtzehn	*eighteen (18)*
neunzehn	*nineteen (19)*
zwanzig	*twenty (20)*

Had a look ☐ **Nearly there** ☐ **Nailed it** ☐

einundzwanzig	*twenty-one (21)*
zweiundzwanzig	*twenty-two (22)*
dreiundzwanzig	*twenty-three (23)*
vierundzwanzig	*twenty-four (24)*
fünfundzwanzig	*twenty-five (25)*
sechsundzwanzig	*twenty-six (26)*
siebenundzwanzig	*twenty-seven (27)*
achtundzwanzig	*twenty-eight (28)*

Had a look ☐ **Nearly there** ☐ **Nailed it** ☐

High-frequency words

neunundzwanzig	twenty-nine (29)		
dreißig	thirty (30)		

Had a look ☐ **Nearly there** ☐ **Nailed it** ☐

vierzig	forty (40)
fünfzig	fifty (50)
sechzig	sixty (60)
siebzig	seventy (70)
achtzig	eighty (80)
neunzig	ninety (90)
hundert	(one) hundred (100)
einhundert	(one) hundred (100)
hunderteins	one hundred and one (101)
hundertzwanzig	one hundred and twenty (120)
zweihundert	two hundred (200)
tausend	one thousand (1,000)
eintausend	one thousand (1,000)
tausendeinhundert	one thousand one hundred (1,100)
elfhundert	one thousand one hundred (1,100)
zweitausend	two thousand (2,000)
(eine) Million	one million (1,000,000)
zwei Millionen	two million (2,000,000)

Had a look ☐ **Nearly there** ☐ **Nailed it** ☐

erster/erste/erstes	first
zweiter/zweite/zweites	second
elfter/elfte/elftes	eleventh
einundzwanzigster/ einundzwanzigste/ einundzwanzigstes	twenty-first

Had a look ☐ **Nearly there** ☐ **Nailed it** ☐

Quantities and measures

viele	many
mehrere	several
genug	enough
ein bisschen	a little
ein Drittel	a third (of)
ein Dutzend	a dozen
eine Dose	a tin (of)
eine Flasche	a bottle (of)
ein Glas	a jar (of)
eine Kiste	a box (of)
eine Packung	a packet (of)
eine Schachtel	a box (of)
eine Scheibe	a slice (of)
ein Stück	a piece (of)
eine Tafel	a bar (of)
eine Tüte	a bag (of)

Had a look ☐ **Nearly there** ☐ **Nailed it** ☐

Some useful connecting words

aber	but
also	so
anstatt	instead
auch	also
außerdem	additionally, moreover
dafür	instead
danach	afterwards
dann	then
deshalb	for this reason
deswegen	for this reason
jedoch	however
nachher	afterwards, later
oder	or
übrigens	by the way, moreover
und	and
vorher	beforehand
weil	because
zuerst	first of all

Had a look ☐ **Nearly there** ☐ **Nailed it** ☐

Time expressions

der Tag(e)	day
der Morgen(–)	morning
der Vormittag(e)	morning
der Nachmittag(e)	afternoon
der Abend(e)	evening
die Nacht (Nächte)	night
Mitternacht	midnight
die Woche(n)	week
das Wochenende(n)	weekend
gestern	yesterday
heute	today
morgen	tomorrow
morgen früh	tomorrow morning
übermorgen	the day after tomorrow
vorgestern	the day before yesterday
die Minute(n)	minute

Had a look ☐ **Nearly there** ☐ **Nailed it** ☐

ab	from
ab und zu	now and then
von Zeit zu Zeit	from time to time
am Anfang	at the start
bald	soon
früh	early
heutzutage	nowadays
immer	always
immer noch	still
jetzt	now
meistens	mostly
nächst–	next
pünktlich	on time
rechtzeitig	on time

High-frequency words

seit	*since*
sofort	*immediately*
spät	*late*
später	*later*
täglich	*every day, daily*
wöchentlich	*weekly*

Had a look ☐ **Nearly there** ☐ **Nailed it** ☐

Times of day

(um) ein Uhr	*(at) one o'clock*
13.00 Uhr	*one o'clock (1 p.m.)*
dreizehn Uhr	*one o'clock (1 p.m.)*
21.00 Uhr	*nine o'clock (9 p.m.)*
einundzwanzig Uhr	*nine o'clock (9 p.m.)*
neun Uhr abends	*nine o'clock in the evening*
genau um 14.00 Uhr	*at exactly two o'clock (2 p.m.)*
genau um vierzehn Uhr	*at exactly two o'clock (2 p.m.)*
gegen ... Uhr	*at about ... o'clock*
ungefähr um ... Uhr	*at about ... o'clock*
es ist 3.05 Uhr	*it is five past three*
es ist drei Uhr fünf	*it is five past three*
fünf vor drei	*five to three*
zehn nach vier	*ten past four*
zehn vor vier	*ten to four*
Viertel vor sechs	*quarter to six*
Viertel nach sieben	*quarter past seven*
halb elf	*half past ten*

Had a look ☐ **Nearly there** ☐ **Nailed it** ☐

Days of the week

Montag	*Monday*
Dienstag	*Tuesday*
Mittwoch	*Wednesday*
Donnerstag	*Thursday*
Freitag	*Friday*
Samstag	*Saturday*
Sonnabend	*Saturday*
Sonntag	*Sunday*
(am) Montag	*(on) Monday*
(am) Montagvormittag	*(on) Monday morning*
(am) Montagabend	*(on) Monday evening*
montags	*on Mondays*
jeden Montag	*every Monday*

Had a look ☐ **Nearly there** ☐ **Nailed it** ☐

Months and seasons

der Monat(e)	*month*
Januar	*January*
Februar	*February*
März	*March*
April	*April*
Mai	*May*
Juni	*June*
Juli	*July*
August	*August*
September	*September*
Oktober	*October*
November	*November*
Dezember	*December*
die Jahreszeit(en)	*season*
(im) Frühling	*(in) spring*
(im) Sommer	*(in) summer*
(im) Herbst	*(in) autumn*
(im) Winter	*(in) winter*

Had a look ☐ **Nearly there** ☐ **Nailed it** ☐

Question words

wann?	*when?*
warum?	*why?*
was für?	*what sort of?*
was?	*what?*
wen? wem?	*whom?*
wer?	*who?, whom?*
wessen?	*whose?*
wie viel(e)?	*how much?, how many?*
wie?	*how?*
wo?	*where?*

Had a look ☐ **Nearly there** ☐ **Nailed it** ☐

Other useful expressions

Es gibt ...	*There is/are ...*
Hier gibt es ...	*Here is/are ...*
Man darf nicht ...	*You are not allowed to ...*
Man muss ...	*You/one must ...*
Wie schreibt man das?	*How do you spell that?*
Was bedeutet das?	*What does that mean?*
Noch einmal?	*Once again?*
Ich verstehe nicht.	*I don't understand.*
Ich weiß es nicht.	*I don't know.*
Es geht mir gut.	*I'm fine.*
Ich bin satt.	*I'm full. / I've had enough (to eat).*
Natürlich!	*Of course!*
In Ordnung!	*OK! (in agreement)*
Mit Vergnügen!	*With pleasure!*
Viel Glück!	*Good luck!*
Schade!	*Too bad! / What a shame!*
Genug davon!	*That's enough!*

Had a look ☐ **Nearly there** ☐ **Nailed it** ☐

Opinions

Meiner Meinung nach ...	*In my opinion ...*
Ich denke, dass ...	*In my opinion ...*
Persönlich ...	*Personally, ...*
Das interessiert mich nicht.	*That doesn't interest me / appeal to me.*
Es ärgert mich.	*It annoys me.*

High-frequency words

Es bringt mich zum Lachen.	It makes me laugh.	die Schweiz	Switzerland
Es gefällt mir.	I like it.	Schottland	Scotland
Es ist mir egal.	I don't mind.	Spanien	Spain
Es kommt darauf an.	It depends.	die Türkei	Turkey
Es lohnt sich nicht.	It's not worth it.	die USA	the United States
Es macht nichts.	It doesn't matter.	die Vereinigten Staaten	the United States
		Wales	Wales

Had a look ☐ Nearly there ☐ Nailed it ☐   Had a look ☐ Nearly there ☐ Nailed it ☐

Other useful words

		### Continents	
ja	yes	Afrika	Africa
nein	no	Asien	Asia
das	that	Australien	Australia
etwas	something	Europa	Europe
ob	whether, if	Nordamerika	North America
wenn	if, when	Südamerika	South America
wie	as, like		
alle	everyone		
jeder	everybody		
jemand	someone		
zum Beispiel	for example		

Had a look ☐ Nearly there ☐ Nailed it ☐   Had a look ☐ Nearly there ☐ Nailed it ☐

		### Nationalities	
das Ding(e)	thing	Amerikaner(in)	American
die Sache(n)	thing	amerikanisch	American
der Gegenstand (-stände)	object	Belgier(in)	Belgian
		belgisch	Belgian
die Form(en)	shape	Brite/Britin	British
die Art(en)	type	britisch	British
die Weise(n)	way	Däne/Dänin	Danish
die Nummer(n)	number	dänisch	Danish
das Mal(e)	time	Deutsche(r)	German
die Zahl(en)	figure, number	deutsch	German
die Mitte(n)	middle	Engländer(in)	English
das Ende(n)	end	englisch	English
Herr ...	Mr ...	Franzose/Französin	French
Frau ...	Mrs ...	französisch	French
		Grieche/Griechin	Greek
		griechisch	Greek
		Inder(in)	Indian
		indisch	Indian
		Ire/Irin	Irish
		irisch	Irish

Had a look ☐ Nearly there ☐ Nailed it ☐

Countries

Had a look ☐ Nearly there ☐ Nailed it ☐

Belgien	Belgium		
Dänemark	Denmark	Italiener(in)	Italian
Deutschland	Germany	italienisch	Italian
England	England	Niederländer(in)	Dutch
Frankreich	France	niederländisch	Dutch
Griechenland	Greece	Österreicher(in)	Austrian
Großbritannien	Great Britain	österreichisch	Austrian
Indien	India	Pakistani	Pakistani
Irland	Ireland	pakistanisch	Pakistani
Italien	Italy	Russe/Russin	Russian
die Niederlande	the Netherlands	russisch	Russian
Österreich	Austria	Schotte/Schottin	Scottish
Polen	Poland	schottisch	Scottish
Russland	Russia	Schweizer(in)	Swiss

High-frequency words

schweizerisch	Swiss
Spanier(in)	Spanish
spanisch	Spanish
Türke/Türkin	Turkish
türkisch	Turkish
Waliser(in)	Welsh
walisisch	Welsh

Had a look ☐ **Nearly there** ☐ **Nailed it** ☐

Places

Bayern	Bavaria
Köln	Cologne
München	Munich
Wien	Vienna
die Alpen	the Alps
der Schwarzwald	the Black Forest
die Donau	the Danube
der Rhein	the Rhine
der Bodensee	Lake Constance
der Ärmelkanal	the English Channel
der Eurotunnel	the Channel Tunnel

Had a look ☐ **Nearly there** ☐ **Nailed it** ☐

Social conventions

Guten Tag!	Good day!
Guten Abend!	Good evening!
Gute Nacht!	Good night!
Grüß Gott!	Hello!
Auf Wiedersehen!	Goodbye!
Bis später!	See you later!
Bis bald!	See you soon!
Bis morgen!	See you tomorrow!
Entschuldigung!	Excuse me!
Hilfe!	Help!
Wie bitte?	I beg your pardon?
Alles Gute!	All the best!
Mit bestem Gruß	Best wishes
bitte	please
danke schön	thank you very much
Bitte schön!	You're welcome!

Had a look ☐ **Nearly there** ☐ **Nailed it** ☐

Language used in dialogues and messages

Rufen Sie mich an!	Call me! (formal)
Ruf mich an!	Call me! (informal)
Kann ich etwas ausrichten?	Can I take a message?
Ich verbinde Sie.	I will put you through.
Ich höre zu.	I'm listening.
Ich bin gleich wieder da.	I'll be right back.
Warten Sie einen Moment.	Wait a moment.

Betreff …	Regarding …
In Bezug auf …	Further to / Following …
Zu Händen von …	For the attention of …

Had a look ☐ **Nearly there** ☐ **Nailed it** ☐

das Telefon(e)	telephone
der Hörer(–)	receiver (telephone)
der Ton (Töne)	tone
die Vorwahl(en)	area code
die Telefonnummer wählen	to dial the number
im Gespräch mit	in communication with
am Apparat	on the line / speaking
der Augenblick(e)	moment
für jetzt	for the moment
falsche Nummer	wrong number
die SMS(–)	text message
simsen	to text
die E-Mail(s)	email
gesandt von	sent by
eigentlich	in fact

Had a look ☐ **Nearly there** ☐ **Nailed it** ☐

Kapitel 1 Wörter

Words I should know for speaking and writing activities

Schulfächer	*School subjects*
Sprachen:	*languages:*
Deutsch	*German*
Englisch	*English*
Französisch	*French*
Spanisch	*Spanish*
Naturwissenschaft(en):	*science(s):*
Biologie	*biology*
Chemie	*chemistry*
Physik	*physics*
Mathe(matik)	*math(ematic)s*
Informatik	*ICT*
Geschichte	*history*
Erdkunde	*geography*
Kunst	*art*
Musik	*music*
Theater	*drama*
Religion	*RE*
Sport	*PE, sport*

Had a look ☐ **Nearly there** ☐ **Nailed it** ☐

Kleidung	*Clothes*
Ich trage (nie) …	*I (never) wear…*
einen Rock	*a skirt*
eine Jeans	*jeans*
eine Hose	*trousers*
eine Jacke	*a jacket*
eine Krawatte	*a tie*
ein Hemd	*a shirt*
ein Kleid	*a dress*
ein T-Shirt	*a T-shirt*
Sportschuhe	*trainers*
Schuhe	*shoes*

Had a look ☐ **Nearly there** ☐ **Nailed it** ☐

Das neue Schuljahr	*The new school year*
In der neunten Klasse freue ich mich (nicht) auf …	*In Year 9, I'm (not) looking forward to …*
den Matheunterricht	*the maths lessons*
die Klassenfahrt	*the class trip*
das Zeugnis	*the report*
die Hausaufgaben	*the homework*
die Klassenarbeiten	*the tests*
die Prüfungen	*the exams*
die Gruppen / Clubs	*the (after-school) groups / clubs*
neue Fächer	*new subjects*
meine Freunde/ Freundinnen	*my friends*
total	*totally*
(echt) sehr	*(really) very*
(gar) nicht	*not (at all)*

nie	*never*
ein bisschen	*a bit*

Had a look ☐ **Nearly there** ☐ **Nailed it** ☐

weil er/sie/es … ist	*because he/she/it is…*
weil sie … sind	*because they are …*
langweilig	*boring*
stressig	*stressful*
schwierig	*difficult*
interessant	*interesting*
einfach	*simple*
prima	*great*
weil …	*because …*
es viele Klassenarbeiten gibt	*there are lots of tests*
wir in die Alpen fahren	*we are going to the Alps*
(Theater) mein Lieblingsfach ist	*(drama) is my favourite subject*
denn …	*because …*
sie sind mir wichtig	*they are important to me*
ich bekomme schlechte / gute Noten	*I get bad / good grades*
ich hatte letztes Jahr ein gutes / schlechtes Zeugnis	*I had a good / bad report last year*
das macht viel Spaß	*it's a lot of fun*

Had a look ☐ **Nearly there** ☐ **Nailed it** ☐

In den Sommerferien	*In the summer holidays*
Ich habe …	*I …*
(neue Bücher) gekauft	*bought (new books)*
(Gitarre) gelernt	*learned (guitar)*
(Fußball) gespielt	*played (football)*
nie (Hausaufgaben) gemacht	*never did (homework)*
immer (eine Mütze) getragen	*always wore (a cap)*
oft (einen Film) gesehen	*often watched (a film)*
Ich bin (in die Alpen) gefahren.	*I went (to the Alps).*
Ich hatte (ein Problem).	*I had (a problem).*
Das war (langweilig).	*That was (boring).*

Had a look ☐ **Nearly there** ☐ **Nailed it** ☐

Schulsachen	*School items*
Was hast du (für das neue Schuljahr) gekauft?	*What have you bought (for the new school year)?*
Ich habe … gekauft.	*I bought …*
einen Bleistift	*a pencil*
einen Kuli	*a ballpoint pen*
einen Radiergummi	*a rubber*
einen Taschenrechner	*a calculator*

Kapitel 1 Wörter

eine Schultasche — *a school bag*
ein Etui — *a pencil case*
Filzstifte — *felt-tip pens*

Had a look ☐ **Nearly there** ☐ **Nailed it** ☐

Ein Schultag / *A school day*

Was hat (die Klasse 9) in der (ersten) Stunde am (Montag)? — *What does (Year 9) have in the (first) lesson on (Monday)?*
Was hast du in der (zweiten) Stunde am (Dienstag)? — *What do you have in the (second) lesson on (Tuesday)?*
erste(n) — *first*
zweite(n) — *second*
dritte(n) — *third*
vierte(n) — *fourth*
fünfte(n) — *fifth*
sechste(n) — *sixth*
siebte(n) — *seventh*
Die Schule beginnt / endet um … — *School starts / ends at …*
nach der Pause — *after the break*
nach der Mittagspause — *after the lunch break*
Wir haben … Stunden pro Tag. — *We have … lessons per day.*
Jede Stunde dauert … Minuten. — *Each lesson lasts … minutes.*
Mein Lieblingsfach ist (Physik). — *My favourite subject is (physics).*
Ich bekomme immer gute Noten. — *I always get good grades.*
Ich mag (Chemie) (nicht). — *I (don't) like (chemistry).*
Ich mache (nicht) gern (Kunst). — *I (don't) like doing (art).*
Um wie viel Uhr? — *At what time?*
Hast du ein Lieblingsfach? — *Do you have a favourite subject?*
Welches Fach? — *Which subject?*

Had a look ☐ **Nearly there** ☐ **Nailed it** ☐

In der Schule / *At school*

der Computerraum — *ICT room*
der Schulhof — *playground*
die Aula — *assembly hall*
die Bibliothek — *library*
die Kantine — *canteen*
die Sporthalle — *sports hall*
das Klassenzimmer — *classroom*
das Labor — *lab(oratory)*
das Lehrerzimmer — *staff room*
die Toiletten — *toilets*

Had a look ☐ **Nearly there** ☐ **Nailed it** ☐

Die Schulordnung / *School rules*

Wir dürfen (nicht) … — *We are (not) allowed to …*
schlagen — *hit*
rauchen — *smoke*
essen — *eat*
trinken — *drink*
Wir dürfen keine Mützen tragen. — *We're not allowed to wear caps.*
Wir dürfen keinen Dialekt sprechen. — *We're not allowed to speak dialect.*
Wir müssen … — *We have to …*
pünktlich sein — *be punctual*
ruhig sein — *be quiet*
(un)gerecht — *(un)just*
(un)fair — *(un)fair*
Ich stimme da (nicht) zu. — *I (don't) agree.*
Du hast recht. — *You are right.*
Ich bin (nicht / ganz) deiner Meinung. — *I (don't / totally) agree with you.*
Nein, das finde ich …, weil … — *No, I find that … because …*
das (schrecklich) ist — *it's (terrible)*
ich das mag — *I like it*
denn … — *because …*
man muss (ruhig) sein — *you have to be (quiet)*
das ist (un)wichtig — *that's (un)important*

Had a look ☐ **Nearly there** ☐ **Nailed it** ☐

Eine Klassenfahrt / *A class trip*

Wir werden auf Austausch fahren. — *We will go on an exchange visit.*
Was werden wir am (Mittwoch) machen? — *What will we do on (Wednesday)?*
Ich werde … / Wir werden … — *I will … / We will …*
an einem Tag an der Schule lernen — *learn at school for a day*
den Abend bei einer Familie verbringen — *spend the evening with a family*
die Stadt besuchen — *visit the town*
in der Stadt bummeln — *stroll around the town*
eine Fahrradtour machen — *go on a cycling tour*
ins Hallenbad gehen — *go to the indoor swimming pool*
das Zirkusmuseum besuchen — *visit the circus museum*
die Sehenswürdigkeiten besichtigen — *visit the sights*
Andenken kaufen — *buy souvenirs*
(wieder) nach Hause fahren — *go home (again)*

Had a look ☐ **Nearly there** ☐ **Nailed it** ☐

14

Extra words I should know for reading and listening activities

Schularbeit — School work

die Fremdsprache(n)	foreign language
Latein	Latin
Technisches Zeichnen	technical drawing
Werken	DT
der Stundenplan	timetable
die Doppelstunde(n)	double lesson
die Durchschnittsnote(n)	average grade
befriedigend	fair
ausreichend	satisfactory
mangelhaft	poor
ungenügend	unsatisfactory
der Notendruck	pressure to achieve good grades
der Erfolg(e)	success
die Leistung(en)	achievement
bestehen*	to pass (exam / test)
das Abitur	German equivalent of A levels
das Abschlusszeugnis	school leaving certificate

Had a look ☐ Nearly there ☐ Nailed it ☐

Die Schulen — Schools

die Grundschule(n)	primary school
die Sekundarschule(n)	secondary school
die Gesamtschule(n)	comprehensive school
die Hauptschule(n)	type of secondary school
die Realschule(n)	type of secondary school
das Gymnasium (Gymnasien)	grammar school
das Internat(e)	boarding school
die Oberstufe	sixth form
die Ganztagsschule**	all-day school
gemischt	mixed

Had a look ☐ Nearly there ☐ Nailed it ☐

In der Schule — At school

das Klassenzimmer(–)	classroom
das Sekretariat*	(school) office, reception
die Turnhalle	gym
der Umkleideraum (–räume)	changing room
die Versammlung(en)	assembly
der Stuhl (Stühle)	chair
die Tafel(n)	(black / white) board
der Tisch(e)	table
die Renovierung(en)	renovation
das Schulnetzwerk(e)**	school network (Wi-Fi)
der Anspitzer	pencil sharpener
der Direktor	headteacher, principal
der Schulleiter	headteacher, principal
der Hausmeister(–)	caretaker
der/die Lehrer(in)	teacher
der/die Schüler(in)	pupil
die Schuluniform(en)	school uniform
das Kleidungsstück(e)	piece of clothing
die Bluse(n)	blouse
das Kleid(er)	dress

Had a look ☐ Nearly there ☐ Nailed it ☐

Auf Austausch — On an exchange

der Austausch	exchange
der/die Austauschpartner(in)	exchange partner
der Ausweis	identity card
die Grenze(n)	border
der Reisepass	passport
der Tagesausflug (–ausflüge)	day trip
die Radtour(en)	cycling tour
der Basketballplatz (–plätze)	basketball court
das Freibad(–bäder)	open-air swimming pool
der Freizeitpark(s)	amusement park
der Sportplatz(–plätze)	sports field, playing field
der Tennisplatz(–plätze)	tennis court
der Internetanschluss (–anschlüsse)	internet connection
das WLAN	Wi-Fi
die Konsole(n)	(games) console
die Katastrophe(n)	catastrophe
mitfahren	to go with
mitnehmen	to take with (you)
reisekrank sein	to be travel sick
in Kontakt bleiben	to keep in touch / contact
wandern	to go hiking

Had a look ☐ Nearly there ☐ Nailed it ☐

⭐ *Watch out for false friends! To say 'to pass an exam' in German, you don't use *passieren* (which means 'to happen'). Instead, you need the verb *bestehen*:

Ich hoffe, ich werde meine Prüfungen bestehen.
I hope I will pass my exams.

Similarly, *Sekretariat* might look like 'secretary', but it's actually the (school) office, or reception.

⭐ **Break unfamiliar words down into their component parts to work out their meaning:

die Ganztagsschule → *ganz* (whole) + *Tag* (day) + *Schule* (school) = whole-day school (or, all-day school)

das Schulnetzwerk → *Schul(e)* (school) + *Netzwerk* (network) = school network

Kapitel 2 Wörter

Words I should know for speaking and writing activities

Freizeitaktivitäten / *Leisure activities*

Sport machen	*to do sport*
Sport treiben	*to do sport*
Fußball spielen	*to play football*
Hockey spielen	*to play hockey*
Basketball spielen	*to play basketball*
Schach spielen	*to play chess*
Karten spielen	*to play cards*
am Computer spielen	*to play on the computer*
auf dem Tablet spielen	*to play on the tablet*
auf dem Handy spielen	*to play on the mobile phone*
Computerspiele spielen	*to play computer games*
Freunde treffen	*to meet friends*
(Zeit) verbringen	*to spend (time)*
ins Kino gehen	*to go to the cinema*
in die Stadt gehen	*to go into town*
Musik machen	*to make music*
Musik hören	*to listen to music*
Bücher lesen	*to read books*
Zeitschriften lesen	*to read magazines*
fernsehen	*to watch TV*
Videos gucken	*to watch videos*
faulenzen	*to laze around*
nichts tun	*to do nothing*

Had a look ☐   Nearly there ☐   Nailed it ☐

Bücher / *Books*

die Biografie(n)	*biography*
der Comic(s)	*comic book*
der Fantasyroman(e)	*fantasy novel*
der Krimi(s)	*detective / crime story*
die Liebesgeschichte(n)	*love story*
das Magazin(e)	*magazine*
das Science-Fiction-Buch(–Bücher)	*sci-fi book*
die Zeitschrift(en)	*magazine*
die Zeitung(en)	*newspaper*

Had a look ☐   Nearly there ☐   Nailed it ☐

Instrumente / *Instruments*

die Blockflöte(n)	*recorder*
die Flöte(n)	*flute*
die Geige(n)	*violin*
die (elektrische) Gitarre(n)	*(electric) guitar*
die Klarinette(n)	*clarinet*
das Keyboard(s)	*keyboard*
das Klavier(e)	*piano*
das Saxofon(e)	*saxophone*
das Schlagzeug(e)	*drums*
die Trompete(n)	*trumpet*
Ich spiele kein Instrument.	*I don't play an instrument.*

Had a look ☐   Nearly there ☐   Nailed it ☐

Musik / *Music*

die Musikrichtung(en)	*type of music*
Ich höre (nicht) gern …	*I (don't) like listening to …*
Ich höre lieber …	*I prefer to listen to …*
Ich höre am liebsten …	*I like listening to … best of all.*
klassische Musik	*classical music*
Opernmusik	*opera*
Popmusik	*pop music*
Reggae	*reggae*
R&B	*R&B*
Rapmusik	*rap*
Heavy Metal	*heavy metal*
Country-und-Western-Musik	*country and western*
Jazzmusik	*jazz*
Livemusik	*live music*
Musik downloaden	*to download music*
die Musiksammlung(en)	*music collection*

Had a look ☐   Nearly there ☐   Nailed it ☐

Film und Fernsehen / *Film and television*

der Film(e)	*film, movie*
der Actionfilm(e)	*action movie*
der Fantasyfilm(e)	*fantasy film*
der Horrorfilm(e)	*horror film*
der Krimi(s)	*detective / crime film*
der Liebesfilm(e)	*romance*
der Science-Fiction-Film(e)	*sci-fi film*
der Thriller(–)	*thriller*
der Zeichentrickfilm(e)	*cartoon*
Ich sehe gern fern.	*I like watching TV.*
das Fernsehen	*television*
der Zuschauer(–)	*viewer*
die Fernsehsendung(en)	*TV programme*
die Dokumentation(en)	*documentary*
die Gameshow(s)	*game show*
die Komödie(n)	*comedy*
die Realityshow(s)	*reality show*
die Serie(n)	*series*
die Nachrichten (pl)	*the news*

Had a look ☐   Nearly there ☐   Nailed it ☐

Ich habe den Film … gefunden.	*I found the film …*
Ich habe die Sendung … gefunden.	*I found the programme …*
Der Film war …	*The film was …*
Die Sendung war …	*The programme was …*
Die Story war …	*The story / plot was …*
Die Schauspieler waren …	*The actors were …*

Kapitel 2 Wörter

Die Charaktere waren …	The characters were …	der Feiertag(e)	public holiday
furchtbar	terrible	das Fest(e)	festival, fair
großartig	great	der Festzug(–züge)	procession
langweilig	boring	die Fete(n)	party
schwach	weak	die Feier(n)	celebration
(un)realistisch	(un)realistic	das Feuerwerk(e)	fireworks (pl)
Ich empfehle den Film / die Sendung, weil …	I recommend the film / programme because …	das Geschenk(e)	present
		der Karneval	carnival
		die Kerze(n)	candle
		die Spezialität(en)	speciality
		das Spielzeug(e) (aus Holz)	(wooden) toy
		die Stimmung(en)	atmosphere
		die Tradition(en)	tradition
		das Volksfest(e)	(traditional) fair
		der Weihnachtsmarkt (–märkte)	Christmas market
		der Weihnachtsschmuck	Christmas decorations

Had a look ☐ **Nearly there** ☐ **Nailed it** ☐

Sport

Ski fahren	to go skiing
snowboarden	to go snowboarding
eislaufen	to ice skate
wandern	to hike
klettern	to climb
schwimmen	to swim
Fahrrad / Rad fahren	to cycle
Handball spielen	to play handball
Tennis spielen	to play tennis
Ich möchte …	I would like …
in den Bergen wandern	to go hiking in the mountains
an den Felsen klettern	to go rock climbing
Ich spiele gern (Fußball).	I like playing (football).
Ich (fahre) gern (Ski).	I like (skiing).
Ich (fahre) nicht gern (Rad).	I (don't) like (cycling).
Ich turne (sehr) gern.	I (very much) like doing gymnastics.
Ich spiele seit (fünf Jahren) (Tennis).	I have been playing (tennis) (for five years).
Ich trainiere (jeden Tag) im Verein.	I train at the club (every day).
Ich trainiere (einmal pro Woche) in einer Mannschaft.	I train in a team (once a week).
Ich möchte bestimmt (Skateboard fahren).	I would definitely like to (go skateboarding).
Ich möchte nie (snowboarden).	I would never like to (go snowboarding).
Ich habe (diese Woche) (Eislaufen) ausprobiert.	I tried (ice skating) (this week).
Ich habe (gestern) (Klettern) ausprobiert.	I tried (climbing) (yesterday).

Had a look ☐ **Nearly there** ☐ **Nailed it** ☐

Feste und Feiertage — Celebrations and holidays

am 24. Dezember (usw.)	on the 24th December (etc.)
feiern	to celebrate
Silvester	New Year's Eve
zu Ostern	at Easter
zu Weihnachten	at Christmas

Had a look ☐ **Nearly there** ☐ **Nailed it** ☐

Kapitel 2 Wörter

Extra words I should know for reading and listening activities

Freizeitaktivitäten — Leisure activities
- sich amüsieren — to have fun
- (sich) entspannen — to relax
- Interesse haben an — to be interested in
- im Internet chatten — to chat online
- im Internet surfen — to surf online
- das Eintrittsgeld — entry fee
- die Eintrittskarte(n) — entry ticket
- der Jugendklub(s) — youth club
- die Unterhaltung — entertainment

Had a look ☐ Nearly there ☐ Nailed it ☐

Musik hören — Listening to music
- die Festplatte(n) — hard drive
- die Kopfhörer (pl) — headphones
- der Lautsprecher(–) — (loud)speaker
- das Lied(er) — song
- der Ton — sound
- die Volksmusik — folk music
- die neunziger Jahre — the nineties
- Platz sparen — to save space
- üben — to practise

Had a look ☐ Nearly there ☐ Nailed it ☐

Film und Fernsehen — Film and TV
- der Abenteuerfilm(e) — adventure film
- der Bildschirm(e) — screen (TV, computer)
- der Fernseher(–) — television (set)
- die Kurzfassung(en) — summary
- die Leinwand(–wände) — (big) screen (in cinema)
- die Originalfassung(en) — original version
- der Sitz(platz) — seat (in cinema, etc.)
- mit Untertiteln — with subtitles
- beeindruckend — impressive
- begabt — talented
- gruselig — creepy, scary
- lebhaft — lively
- unterhaltsam — entertaining
- witzig — witty

Had a look ☐ Nearly there ☐ Nailed it ☐

Sport — Sport
- angeln — to fish
- fechten — to fence
- kegeln — (nine-pin) bowling
- rennen — to run
- ringen — to wrestle
- rodeln — to go tobogganing
- Rollschuh laufen — to go roller skating
- rudern — to row
- schießen — to shoot
- segeln — to sail
- tauchen — to dive
- turnen — to do gymnastics
- der Federball — badminton
- der Korbball — netball
- die Sportart(en) — type of sport

Had a look ☐ Nearly there ☐ Nailed it ☐

Feste und Feiertage — Celebrations and holidays
- der Neujahrstag — New Year's Day
- der Karfreitag — Good Friday
- der Ostersonntag — Easter Sunday
- der Maifeiertag — May Day
- der Muttertag — Mother's Day
- der Tag der Deutschen Einheit — Day of German Unity
- der Nikolaustag — St Nicholas' Day (6th December)
- das Osterei(er) — Easter egg
- der Osterhase — Easter bunny
- die Wiedervereinigung* — reunification
- die Einladung(en) — invitation
- die Rede(n) — speech
- der Umzug(–züge) — street procession
- einladen — to invite
- schmücken — to decorate
- sich verkleiden — to dress up

Had a look ☐ Nearly there ☐ Nailed it ☐

Auf dem Weihnachtsmarkt — At the Christmas market
- der Adventskranz — advent wreath
- der Weihnachtsbaum(–bäume) — Christmas tree
- das Weihnachtslied(er) — Christmas carol
- die Wollmütze(n) — woolly hat
- der Imbiss(e) — snack
- die Bratwurst(–würste) — fried sausage
- der Glühwein — mulled wine
- der Kinderpunsch — non-alcoholic punch
- der Lebkuchen — gingerbread
- die Waffel(n) — waffle
- kandierte Äpfel — candied apples
- geröstete Mandeln — roasted almonds

Had a look ☐ Nearly there ☐ Nailed it ☐

> *Don't be daunted by long, tricky-looking words. Look carefully at the words they are made up of and try to work out the meaning based on the words you know.
>
> *die Wiedervereinigung*
> You know that *wieder* means 'again' and *der Verein* is 'club' (i.e. somewhere where people come together), so *Wiedervereinigung* is literally 'the coming together again', or 'reunification'.
>
> *Am 3. Oktober feiert man die Wiedervereinigung Deutschlands.* On 3rd October, we celebrate the reunification of Germany.

Kapitel 3 Wörter

Words I should know for speaking and writing activities

Charaktereigen-schaften	Personal characteristics
Er/Sie ist (nicht) …	He/She is (not)…
aktiv	active
cool	cool
dynamisch	dynamic
fleißig	hard-working
frech	cheeky
freundlich	friendly
intelligent	intelligent
kreativ	creative
langweilig	boring
lustig	funny
nett	nice
originell	original
sportlich	sporty
toll	great
ziemlich	quite
sehr	very
nie	never
nicht	not
relativ	relatively
total	totally

Had a look ☐ Nearly there ☐ Nailed it ☐

Aussehen	Appearance
Er/Sie hat … Haare.	He/She has … hair.
blonde	blonde
braune	brown
schwarze	black
rote	red
lange	long
kurze	short
Er/Sie hat … Augen.	He/She has … eyes.
graue	grey
blaue	blue
grüne	green
Er/Sie trägt …	He/She wears …
eine (modische) Brille	(trendy) glasses
eine (coole) Sonnenbrille	(cool) sunglasses
Er hat einen (großen) Bart.	He has a (big) beard.
Er/Sie ist …	He/She is …
schlank	slim
groß	big, tall
klein	small, short

Had a look ☐ Nearly there ☐ Nailed it ☐

Wie ist ein guter Freund/eine gute Freundin?
What makes a good friend?

Ein guter Freund/Eine gute Freundin …	A good friend …
muss Zeit für mich haben	must have time for me
muss sympathisch sein	must be nice
muss mich immer unterstützen	must always support me
muss viel Geduld haben	must have lots of patience
muss die gleichen Interessen haben	must have the same interests
kann mit mir über alles reden	can talk to me about anything
darf nicht eifersüchtig sein	isn't allowed to be jealous
Das ist für mich …	That is … to me.
nicht wichtig	not important
wichtig	important
sehr wichtig	very important
die Kommunikation	communication

Had a look ☐ Nearly there ☐ Nailed it ☐

Beziehungen	Relationships
Ich verstehe mich gut mit …	I get on well with …
Ich verstehe mich nicht so gut mit …	I don't get on so well with …
meiner Mutter	my mother
meinem Vater	my father
meiner Stiefmutter	my stepmother
meinem Stiefvater	my stepfather
meinen Eltern	my parents
meiner Schwester	my sister
meinem Bruder	my brother
meiner Halbschwester	my half-sister
meinem Halbbruder	my half-brother
meinen Geschwistern	my siblings
meiner Großmutter	my grandmother
meinem Großvater	my grandfather
meiner Oma	my grandma
meinem Opa	my grandpa
meinen Großeltern	my grandparents
meiner Tante	my aunt
meinem Onkel	my uncle
meinen Cousins/Cousinen	my cousins

Had a look ☐ Nearly there ☐ Nailed it ☐

… weil er/sie … ist.	… because he/she is …
dynamisch	dynamic
eifersüchtig	jealous
langweilig	boring
launisch	moody
nervig	annoying
streng	strict
sympathisch	kind, nice
… weil er/sie … (viel / keine) Geduld hat	… because he/she … has (a lot of / no) patience

Kapitel 3 Wörter

(immer / nie) Zeit für mich hat	(always / never) has time for me	einladen	to invite
mich unterstützt	supports me	einstellen	to take on, to appoint
mich nicht unterstützt	doesn't support me	stattfinden	to take place
mir auf die Nerven geht	gets on my nerves	teilnehmen	to take part
		vorbereiten	to prepare
		heiraten	to get married
		getrennt	separated
		Sie lassen sich scheiden.	They are getting divorced.

Had a look ☐   Nearly there ☐   Nailed it ☐

Wir/Sie haben eine tolle Beziehung.	We/They have a great relationship.	Für mich ist die Ehe (nicht) sehr wichtig.	Marriage is (not) very important to me.
Ich streite mich mit (ihr).	I argue with (her).	Ich finde eine Hochzeit …	I find a wedding …
Er/Sie streitet sich mit (ihm).	He/She argues with (him).	Meiner Meinung nach ist eine Hochzeit …	In my opinion a wedding is …
Sie streiten sich mit (ihnen).	They argue with (them).	sehr romantisch	very romantic
Ich werde mich mit (…) besser verstehen.	I will get on better with (…).	altmodisch	old-fashioned
Er/Sie sagt, …	He/She says …	eine Geldverschwendung	a waste of money
Sie sagen, …	They say …	die Ehe	marriage
ich mache nicht genug Hausaufgaben	I don't do enough homework	die Scheidung	divorce

Had a look ☐   Nearly there ☐   Nailed it ☐

ich verbringe zu viel Zeit (mit dem Handy / vor dem Fernseher)	I spend too much time (on my mobile phone / in front of the TV)		
ich darf (den Computer / mein Handy) nicht benutzen	I'm not allowed to use (the computer / my mobile phone)	**Dein Leben jetzt und als Kind**	**Your life now and as a child**
ich darf nicht (Fußball spielen / ausgehen)	I'm not allowed to (play football / go out)	Als ich vier Jahre alt war, konnte ich …	When I was four years old, I could…
		Rad fahren	ride a bike
		(nicht) sehr gut schwimmen	(not) swim very well

Had a look ☐   Nearly there ☐   Nailed it ☐

		(schon) Spanisch sprechen	(already) speak Spanish
Meine perfekte Hochzeit	**My perfect wedding**	Als ich ein Kind war, musste ich …	When I was a child, I had to …
die Blumen (pl)	flowers	immer zu Hause helfen	always help at home
das Brautkleid(er)	wedding dress	um 20:00 Uhr zu Hause sein	be home by 8 p.m.
der Ehering(e)	wedding ring	jeden Abend meine Hausaufgaben machen	do my homework every evening
die Einladung(en)	invitation	früher ins Bett gehen	go to bed earlier
der Fotograf(en)	photographer	Als ich ein Kind war, musste ich keine Hausaufgaben machen.	When I was a child, I didn't have to do homework.
der Gast (Gäste)	guest		
das Hochzeitsauto(s)	wedding car		
der Hochzeitstag(e)	wedding day, wedding anniversary	Als ich jünger war, durfte ich …	When I was younger, I was allowed to …
die Hochzeitstorte(n)	wedding cake	fernsehen	watch TV
die Kirche(n)	church	am Computer spielen	play on the computer
die Location	venue	allein in die Schule gehen	go to school on my own
die Tischrede(n)	speech		
die Verlobte(n)	fiancée	Als ich jünger war, durfte ich …	When I was younger, I was not allowed to …
der Verlobte(n)	fiancé	keine Zeit mit meinen Freunden verbringen	spend time with my friends
die zivile Partnerschaft(en)	civil partnership	am Wochenende nicht mit meinen Freunden in die Stadt gehen	go into town at the weekend with my friends

Had a look ☐   Nearly there ☐   Nailed it ☐

anschaffen	to buy, to get
aussuchen	to choose
auswählen	to select

Kapitel 3 Wörter

nicht zu spät nach Hause kommen	come home too late
am Abend nicht mit Freunden ins Kino gehen	go to the cinema with friends in the evening

Had a look ☐   **Nearly there** ☐   **Nailed it** ☐

Jetzt kann ich …	Now I can …
Am Wochenende darf ich (nicht) …	At the weekend I am (not) allowed to …
Am Abend muss ich …	In the evening I must …
früh ins Bett gehen	go to bed early
spät ins Bett gehen	go to bed late
viele Hausaufgaben machen	do lots of homework
ins Kino gehen	go to the cinema
einkaufen gehen	go shopping
in den Park gehen	go to the park
Zeit mit Freunden verbringen	spend time with friends
(sehr gut) Fußball spielen	play football (very well)
viel trainieren	train a lot
online chatten	chat online
online surfen	surf online
Am Abend muss ich …	In the evening I don't have to …
keine Hausaufgaben machen	do homework
Das finde ich …	I find that …
viel besser	much better
fair	fair
unfair	unfair

Had a look ☐   **Nearly there** ☐   **Nailed it** ☐

Kapitel 3 Wörter

Extra words I should know for reading and listening activities

Charaktereigenschaften und Aussehen	*Personal characteristics and appearance*
die Persönlichkeit(en)	personality
egoistisch*	selfish
ehrlich	honest
ernst	serious
gemein*	mean
glatt	straight, smooth
hilfsbereit	helpful
höflich	polite
hübsch	pretty
humorlos*	humourless, without a sense of humour
humorvoll*	humorous, witty
lockig	curly
schüchtern	shy
selbstständig	independent
still	quiet
unordentlich	messy
unternehmungslustig	adventurous, likes doing lots of things

Had a look ☐ Nearly there ☐ Nailed it ☐

Freundschaften	*Friendships*
der Freundeskreise(e)	circle of friends
das Geheimnis(–nisse)	secret
die Kommunikation	communication
die Priorität(en)	priority
der Typ(en)	type, person, bloke
die Unterstützung	support
auskommen mit	to get on with

Had a look ☐ Nearly there ☐ Nailed it ☐

Beziehungen	*Relationships*
die Kindheit	childhood
der Konflikt(e)	conflict
das Verhältnis(–nisse)	relationship
Ich kann … nicht leiden.	I can't stand …
sich ärgern	to be annoyed
sich entschuldigen	to apologise
erlauben	to allow
sich fühlen**	to feel
sich kümmern um	to look after
sorgen für	to care for, to look after
vergeben	to forgive

Had a look ☐ Nearly there ☐ Nailed it ☐

Familienmitglieder	*Family members*
der/die Erwachsene	adult
der Ehemann	husband
der Mann	man, husband
die Ehefrau	wife
die Frau	woman, wife
der/die Jugendliche	youth, young person
das Kind(er)	child
das Einzelkind(er)	only child
das Enkelkind(er)	grandchild
das Baby(s)	baby
der Sohn (Söhne)	son
die Tochter (Töchter)	daughter
der Schwiegersohn	son-in-law
die Schwiegertochter	daughter-in-law
der Schwager	brother-in-law
die Schwägerin	sister-in-law
der Neffe(n)	nephew
die Nichte(n)	niece
der Zwilling(e)	twin

Had a look ☐ Nearly there ☐ Nailed it ☐

Meine perfekte Hochzeit	*My perfect wedding*
die Dekoration(en)	decoration
das Hochzeitsmenü(s)	wedding menu
der Tanzboden(–böden)	dance floor
die Zeremonie(n)	ceremony
seine Liebe beweisen	to prove your love

Had a look ☐ Nearly there ☐ Nailed it ☐

Familienstand	*Marital status*
single	single
ledig	unmarried
unverheiratet	unmarried
verliebt	in love
verlobt	engaged
verheiratet	married
getrennt	separated
geschieden	divorced
sich verloben	to get engaged
heiraten	to get married
sich trennen	to separate, to split up
sich scheiden lassen	to get divorced

Had a look ☐ Nearly there ☐ Nailed it ☐

⭐ *Look for cognates and near-cognates when working out meanings of new words.

Humorvoll looks similar to the two English words 'humour' and 'full', and means 'humorous'. And *humorlos* means 'humourless'.

Can you see the link between *gemein* and 'mean', or *egoistisch* and 'selfish' (or 'egotistical')?

⭐ **Don't mistake *sich fühlen* for *fühlen*. Both translate as 'to feel', but *sich fühlen* relates to <u>how</u> you feel (yourself), *fühlen* relates to <u>what</u> you feel or sense.

*Ich **fühle mich** gut.* I feel fine.
*Ich **fühle** einen Schmerz.* I feel a pain.

Words I should know for speaking and writing activities

Zu Hause	*At home*
das Arbeitszimmer	*study*
das Badezimmer	*bathroom*
der Dachboden	*attic, loft*
die Dusche	*shower*
das Esszimmer	*dining room*
die Garage	*garage*
der Garten	*garden*
die Küche	*kitchen*
das Schlafzimmer	*bedroom*
das Wohnzimmer	*sitting room*
der Flur	*hall, corridor*

Had a look ☐   **Nearly there** ☐   **Nailed it** ☐

Ich wohne (seit vier Jahren) …	*I have been living … (for four years).*
in einer Kleinstadt	*in a small town*
in einer Großstadt	*in a city*
in der Stadtmitte	*in the town centre*
am Stadtrand	*on the outskirts of town, in the suburbs*
auf dem Land	*in the countryside*
in einem Einfamilienhaus	*in a detached house*
in einer Doppelhaushälfte	*in a semi-detached house*
in einem Reihenhaus	*in a terraced house*
in einem Hochhaus	*in a high-rise building*
in einem Wohnblock	*in a block of flats*
Im Erdgeschoss gibt es …	*On the ground floor there is …*
Im ersten Stock gibt es …	*On the first floor there is …*
Wir haben keinen Tennisplatz.	*We don't have a tennis court.*

Had a look ☐   **Nearly there** ☐   **Nailed it** ☐

Auf Austausch	*On an exchange visit*
Herzlich willkommen in (Deutschland)!	*Welcome to (Germany)!*
Wie geht's dir / Ihnen?	*How are you?*
Wie bitte?	*Pardon?*
Ich verstehe deine / Ihre Frage nicht.	*I don't understand your question.*
Hast du / Haben Sie Hunger?	*Are you hungry?*
Hast du / Haben Sie Durst?	*Are you thirsty?*
Kannst du / Können Sie bitte langsamer sprechen?	*Can you speak more slowly, please?*
Kannst du / Können Sie das bitte wiederholen?	*Can you repeat that, please?*

Was bedeutet 'Hausschuhe'?	*What does 'Hausschuhe' mean?*
Wie heißt 'Wi-Fi-Code' auf Deutsch?	*How do you say 'WiFi code' in German?*

Had a look ☐   **Nearly there** ☐   **Nailed it** ☐

Man muss in der Ruhezeit ruhig sein.	*We must be quiet during 'quiet time'.*
die Hausordnung	*house rules*
die Mittagsruhe	*quiet time at midday*
die Ruhezeit	*quiet time*
Man darf im Schlafzimmer keine laute Musik spielen.	*We are not allowed to play loud music in the bedroom.*
Man darf kein Instrument üben.	*We are not allowed to practise an instrument.*
Man darf nicht mit dem Ball spielen.	*We are not allowed to play ball games.*
Man darf nie das Auto vor der Garage waschen.	*We are never allowed to wash the car in front of the garage.*
Am Feiertag / Den ganzen Tag ist Ruhezeit!	*On a bank holiday / The whole day it is quiet time!*

Had a look ☐   **Nearly there** ☐   **Nailed it** ☐

Der Tagesablauf	*Daily routine*
an einem Schultag	*on a school day*
am Wochenende	*at the weekend*
täglich	*daily*
am Abend / Nachmittag	*in the evening / afternoon*
nach der Schule / dem Abendessen	*after school / dinner*
aufstehen	*to get up*
frühstücken	*to have breakfast*
abfahren	*to leave*
fernsehen	*to watch TV*
sich setzen	*to sit down, to take a seat*
sich an den Computer setzen	*to sit down at the computer*
am Computer sitzen	*to sit at the computer*
sich amüsieren	*to have a good time*
sich langweilen	*to be bored*
sich mit Freunden treffen	*to meet up with friends*
… Stunden in der Schule verbringen	*to spend … hours at school*

Had a look ☐   **Nearly there** ☐   **Nailed it** ☐

Essen und trinken	*Eating and drinking*
Das Frühstück / Mittagessen / Abendessen / Abendbrot essen wir um …	*We eat breakfast / lunch / dinner at …*
Ich esse / Wir essen …	*I / We eat …*

Kapitel 4 Wörter

K 4

23

Kapitel 4 Wörter

auf der Terrasse	on the terrace / patio
bei uns im Esszimmer	at home in the dining room
auf dem Weg zur Schule	on the way to school
vor dem Fernseher	in front of the TV
Das hat … geschmeckt.	It tasted …
ekelhaft / schrecklich	disgusting / dreadful
köstlich / wunderbar / lecker	delicious / wonderful / tasty
salzig / süß / würzig	salty / sweet / spicy
auswählen	to choose
einkaufen	to buy, to shop
vorbereiten	to prepare

Had a look ☐ **Nearly there** ☐ **Nailed it** ☐

das Brot	bread
der Käse	cheese
die Kartoffelchips (pl)	crisps
die Suppe	soup
die Hauptspeise	main course
der Braten	roast (meat)
die Currywurst	sausage with curry sauce
der Fisch	fish
das Schnitzel	schnitzel, escalope
ein gemischter Salat	mixed salad
das Spiegelei(er)	fried egg
die Wurst	sausage
(mit) Kartoffeln / Reis / Pommes	(with) potatoes / rice / chips
die Nachspeise	dessert
das Eis	ice cream
das Gebäck	baked goods, pastries
der Keks(e)	biscuit
die Torte(n)	gâteau, flan
der Zucchinikuchen	courgette cake
der Pampelmusensaft	grapefruit juice
der Tee	tea
die (Voll-)Milch	(full-fat) milk

Had a look ☐ **Nearly there** ☐ **Nailed it** ☐

Obst und Gemüse / Fruit and vegetables

das Obst	fruit
das Gemüse	vegetables
die Gurke(n)	cucumber
die Karotte(n)	carrot
der Kohl(e)	cabbage
die Paprika(s)	pepper
die Tomate(n)	tomato
die Zwiebel(n)	onion
der Apfel (Äpfel)	apple
die Banane(n)	banana
die Birne(n)	pear
die Erdbeere(n)	strawberry
die Orange(n)	orange
der Pfirsich(e)	peach

Had a look ☐ **Nearly there** ☐ **Nailed it** ☐

Lebst du gesund? / Do you live healthily?

Mein Lieblingssport ist …	My favourite sport is …
Fußball	football
Leichtathletik	athletics
Turnen	gymnastics
Mein Vorbild ist …	My role model is …
ein(e) Athlet(in)	an athlete
ein(e) Fußballspieler(in)	a footballer
ein(e) Schwimmer(in)	a swimmer
Er/Sie …	He/She …
ist begabt	is talented
trainiert hart	trains hard
hat viele Medaillen gewonnen	has won lots of medals
Für meine Fitness …	To keep fit …
gehe ich joggen	I go jogging
gehe ich schwimmen	I go swimming
mache ich Muskeltraining	I do weight training
Ich esse sehr gesund.	I eat very healthily.
Ich esse ziemlich ungesund.	I eat quite unhealthily.
Ich esse Obst und Gemüse.	I eat fruit and vegetables.
Ich esse täglich Fastfood.	I eat fast food every day.
die Diät(en)	diet
übergewichtig	overweight

Had a look ☐ **Nearly there** ☐ **Nailed it** ☐

Soziale Netzwerke und Technologie / Social media and technology

Wie kommunizierst du am liebsten?	How do you most like to communicate?
Ich nutze soziale Netzwerke.	I use social networks.
Ich simse (meinen Eltern).	I text (my parents).
Ich sende E-Mails.	I send emails.
Ich telefoniere per Internet.	I call via the internet.
Ich rufe (meine Freunde) vom Handy an.	I call (my friends) on my mobile.
Ich habe persönliche Gespräche.	I have face-to-face conversations.
…, wenn …	… if …
ich mich langweile	I'm bored
ich mit meinen Freunden rede / spreche	I talk to my friends
ich spät bin	I'm late
ich unterwegs bin	I'm on the way / out and about

Had a look ☐ **Nearly there** ☐ **Nailed it** ☐

Kapitel 4 Wörter

Das ist …	That is …
nützlich	useful
lustig	funny
unterhaltsam	entertaining
wichtig	important
praktisch	practical
Das macht Spaß.	That's fun.
online / im Internet chatten	to chat online
im Internet surfen	to surf online
Fotos hochladen	to upload photos
Musik herunterladen	to download music
der Bildschirm	screen
der Desktop-PC	desktop computer, PC
die Digitalkamera	digital camera
das Handy	mobile phone
der MP3-Player	MP3 player
der Streaming-Dienst	streaming service
das Smart-TV	smart TV
das Tablet	tablet
die Konsole	console

Had a look ☐ **Nearly there** ☐ **Nailed it** ☐

Vor- und Nachteile der Technologie
Advantages and disadvantages of technology

Ich finde es positiv / negativ, dass …	I find it positive / negative that …
Ein großer Vorteil der Technologie ist, dass …	A big advantage of technology is that …
Ein großer Nachteil ist, dass …	A big disadvantage is that …
Es gibt Vorteile und Nachteile.	There are advantages and disadvantages.
einerseits	on the one hand
auf der anderen Seite	on the other hand
Man langweilt sich nie.	You never get bored.
Man amüsiert sich sehr gut am Bildschirm.	You entertain yourself very well on screen.
Technologie ist extrem teuer.	Technology is extremely expensive.
Man bleibt mit Leuten in Kontakt.	You stay in contact with people.
Man ist nicht so oft draußen aktiv.	You're not active outside so often.
Man findet Informationen schnell online.	You find information quickly online.
Das Internet führt manchmal zu Internet-Mobbing.	The internet sometimes leads to cyberbullying.
Das persönliche Leben bleibt nie privat.	Your personal life never stays private.

Had a look ☐ **Nearly there** ☐ **Nailed it** ☐

25

Kapitel 4 Wörter

Extra words I should know for reading and listening activities

Zu Hause / At home

die Decke(n)	ceiling
der Eingang(–gänge)	entrance
die Etage(n)	floor, storey
der Fußboden	floor (ground)
die Heizung	heating
die Mauer(n)	wall (outside)
der Rasen(–)	lawn
die Treppe*	(flight of) stairs, staircase
die Tür(en)	door
die Wand (Wände)	wall (inside)
der Wintergarten	conservatory
aufräumen	to tidy up
mähen	to mow (lawn)
sauber machen	to clean
möbliert	furnished
renoviert	renovated

Had a look ☐ Nearly there ☐ Nailed it ☐

Möbel* / Furniture

das Mobiliar*	furnishings (pl)
das Etagenbett	bunk bed
die Kommode(n)	chest of drawers
der Nachttisch(e)	bedside table
das Regal(e)	shelf
die Schublade(n)	drawer
der Schuhschrank (–schränke)	shoe cupboard
die Badewanne(n)	bathtub
das Waschbecken(–)	washbasin
der Backofen(–öfen)	oven
der Herd(e)	cooker
das Kochfeld(er)	hob
der Kühlschrank (–schränke)	fridge
die Mikrowelle(n)	microwave
die Waschmaschine(n)	washing machine
der Spiegel(–)	mirror
der Teppich(e)	carpet
der Vorhang(–hänge)	curtain

Had a look ☐ Nearly there ☐ Nailed it ☐

Lebst du gesund? / Do you live healthily?

die Bundesliga	German federal league
der Kampf (Kämpfe)	fight
der/die Trainer(in)	coach
das Turnier(e)	tournament
der Wettkampf (–kämpfe)	competition
bewundern	to admire
inspirieren	to inspire

Had a look ☐ Nearly there ☐ Nailed it ☐

Soziale Netzwerke und Technologie / Social media and technology

der Anrufbeantworter(–)	(telephone) answering machine
der Drucker(–)	printer
der Klingelton(e)	ringtone
die Medien (pl)	media
das Netz	net
das Postfach(–fächer)	mail box (email)
das Smartphone(s)	smartphone
die Smartuhr(en)	smart watch
die Startseite	homepage (internet)
der Telefonanruf(e)	telephone call
anrufen	to call, to ring
(aus)drucken	to print (out)
eingeben	to enter (data into computer / phone)
empfangen	to receive
löschen	to delete
speichern	to save (data on computer)

Had a look ☐ Nearly there ☐ Nailed it ☐

Vor- und Nachteile der Technologie / Advantages and disadvantages of technology

die Daten (pl)	data
die Entwicklung(en)	development
die Gefahr(en)	danger
der Missbrauch (–bräuche)	abuse
das Risiko (Risiken)	risk
der Schutz	protection
die Schwierigkeit(en)	difficulty
entwickeln	to develop
funktionieren	to work
missbrauchen	to abuse
teilen	to share
lehrreich	informative, instructive, educational
verboten	forbidden

Had a look ☐ Nearly there ☐ Nailed it ☐

⭐ *Look out for nouns which are singular in German but plural in English, and vice versa:

die Treppe (singular) → (flight of) stairs

das Mobiliar (singular) → furnishings

die Möbel (plural) → furniture

Kapitel 5 Wörter

Words I should know for speaking and writing activities

Verkehrsmittel	***Forms of transport***
Ich fahre ...	*I travel ...*
mit dem Zug / Bus / Auto / Rad	*by train / bus / car / bike*
mit der U-Bahn / S-Bahn / Straßenbahn	*by underground / urban railway / tram*
Ich fliege mit dem Flugzeug.	*I fly.*
Ich gehe zu Fuß.	*I go on foot. / I walk.*

Had a look ☐ Nearly there ☐ Nailed it ☐

Hotelzimmer reservieren	***Booking hotel rooms***
Ich möchte ... reservieren.	*I would like to reserve ...*
ein Einzelzimmer	*a single room*
zwei Doppelzimmer	*two double rooms*
für eine Nacht	*for one night*
für zwei Nächte vom 8. bis 10. Januar	*for two nights from 8 to 10 January*
Möchten Sie ... reservieren?	*Would you like to reserve ...?*
einen Parkplatz	*a parking space*
ein Zimmer mit Aussicht	*a room with a view*
Gibt es WLAN / ein Restaurant im Hotel?	*Is there Wi-Fi / a restaurant in the hotel?*
Wann ist das Restaurant geöffnet?	*When is the restaurant open?*
Um wie viel Uhr gibt es Frühstück?	*What time is breakfast?*

Had a look ☐ Nearly there ☐ Nailed it ☐

Komparative	***Comparatives***
bequemer	*more comfortable*
besser	*better*
billiger	*cheaper*
größer	*bigger*
länger	*longer*
langsamer	*slower*
näher	*nearer*
praktischer	*more practical*
schneller	*quicker*
teurer	*more expensive*
umweltfreundlicher	*more environmentally friendly*
lieber	*prefer*

Had a look ☐ Nearly there ☐ Nailed it ☐

Superlative	***Superlatives***
am besten	*best*
am bequemsten	*most comfortable*
am billigsten	*cheapest*
am einfachsten	*easiest*
am größten	*biggest*
am längsten	*longest*
am nächsten	*nearest*
am schnellsten	*quickest*
am teuersten	*most expensive*
am umweltfreundlichsten	*most environmentally friendly*
am wichtigsten	*most important*
am liebsten	*like the most*

Had a look ☐ Nearly there ☐ Nailed it ☐

Fahrkarten kaufen	***Buying train tickets***
Ich möchte eine Fahrkarte nach Berlin, bitte.	*I'd like a ticket to Berlin, please.*
Einfach oder hin und zurück?	*Single or return?*
Wann fährt der nächste Zug ab?	*When does the next train leave?*
Der Zug fährt um 12:51 Uhr ab.	*The train leaves at 12:51.*
Von welchem Gleis?	*From which platform?*
Vom Gleis 22.	*From platform 22.*
Wann kommt der Zug an?	*When does the train arrive?*
Der Zug kommt um 19:18 Uhr in Berlin an.	*The train arrives in Berlin at 19:18.*

Had a look ☐ Nearly there ☐ Nailed it ☐

Ferienunterkunft	***Holiday accommodation***
das Hotel(s)	*hotel*
das Gasthaus(-häuser)	*guest house, bed and breakfast*
die Ferienwohnung(en)	*holiday apartment*
die Jugendherberge(n)	*youth hostel*
der Campingplatz (-plätze)	*campsite*
Ich möchte ... übernachten.	*I would like to stay ...*
auf diesem Campingplatz	*on this campsite*
in dieser Ferienwohnung	*in this holiday apartment*
in dieser Jugendherberge	*in this youth hostel*
in diesem Hotel / Gasthaus	*in this hotel / guest house*
Es gibt ...	*There is ...*
einen Computerraum	*a computer room*
einen Spieleraum	*a games / play room*
eine gute Aussicht	*a good view*
eine Sauna	*a sauna*
ein Freibad	*an open-air swimming pool*
Er/Sie/Es ist ...	*It is ...*
praktisch	*practical*

27

Kapitel 5 Wörter

ideal	ideal
laut	noisy
schön	lovely

Had a look ☐ **Nearly there** ☐ **Nailed it** ☐

Ich habe (in diesem Hotel) übernachtet.	I stayed (in this hotel).
Das Zimmer war …	The room was …
klein	small
groß	big
(un)bequem	(un)comfortable
schmutzig	dirty
Es gab …	There was …
kein WLAN	no Wi-Fi
viel Lärm	a lot of noise
Es waren Haare in der Dusche.	There were hairs in the shower.
Ich habe eine Maus … gesehen.	I saw a mouse …
unter dem Bett	under the bed
im Restaurant	in the restaurant
Jede Nacht habe ich die Discomusik gehört.	I heard the disco music every night.
Ich werde (nie) wieder hier übernachten.	I will (never) stay here again.

Had a look ☐ **Nearly there** ☐ **Nailed it** ☐

Wegbeschreibungen	**Directions**
Entschuldige, bitte. / Entschuldigen Sie, bitte.	Excuse me, please.
Wo ist der/die/das …?	Where is the …?
Wie komme ich zu …?	How do I get to …?
Fahr / Fahren Sie …	Go …
mit dem Bus	by bus
mit der U-Bahn-Linie 1	by underground line 1
Geh / Gehen Sie …	Go …
rechts / links / geradeaus	right / left / straight on
bis (zum Dom) …	until (the cathedral) …
über …	over …
an der Ecke rechts	right at the corner
an der Kreuzung links	left at the crossroads
Nimm / Nehmen Sie …	Take …
die erste / zweite Straße links	the first / second road on the left
Überquer / Überqueren Sie …	Cross …
die Ampel(n)	the traffic lights
die Kreuzung	the crossroads
den Platz	the square
Es ist auf der (rechten) Seite.	It's on the (right).
das Museum (Museen)	museum
das Rathaus(–häuser)	town hall
das Theater(–)	theatre

der Dom	cathedral
der Rathausplatz (–plätze)	town hall square
die Oper(n)	opera house

Had a look ☐ **Nearly there** ☐ **Nailed it** ☐

Essen	**Eating**
die Kneipe(n)	pub, bar
das Café(s)	café
das Restaurant(s)	restaurant
der Schnellimbiss(e)	snack bar
die Vorspeise(n)	starter
die Hauptspeise(n)	main course
die Nachspeise(n)	dessert
das Tagesgericht	daily special
die Beilage(n)	side dish
das Getränk(e)	drink
die Champignons	mushrooms
der Gemüsestrudel	vegetable strudel

Had a look ☐ **Nearly there** ☐ **Nailed it** ☐

die Kartoffelsuppe	potato soup
der Lammrücken	rump of lamb
die Rindsuppe	consommé, beef soup
das Sauerkraut	sauerkraut, pickled cabbage
der Wursteller	cold sausage platter
das Wiener Schnitzel	breaded schnitzel, escalope
der Apfelstrudel	apple strudel
die Eissorte	ice cream flavour
die Sachertorte	Sacher torte
das Bier (vom Fass)	(draught) beer
der Fruchtsaft	fruit juice
der Wein	wine

Had a look ☐ **Nearly there** ☐ **Nailed it** ☐

Im Restaurant	**In the restaurant**
Wir möchten bitte einen Tisch für vier Personen.	We would like a table for four people.
Der Tisch …	The table …
hat keine Aussicht	doesn't have a view
ist in der Ecke	is in the corner
ist zu klein	is too small
Dieser Löffel ist sehr schmutzig.	This spoon is very dirty.
Es ist ein Haar in diesem Salat.	There is a hair in this salad.
Dieser Wursteller war sehr fettig.	This sausage platter was very fatty.
Das war …	That was …
unappetitlich	unappetising
zu würzig / salzig	too spicy / salty
Ich möchte mich beschweren.	I would like to complain.

Kapitel 5 Wörter

Ich werde (die Suppe) nicht bezahlen. — *I won't pay for (the soup).*
Wir werden in ein anderes Restaurant gehen. — *We will go to another restaurant.*
Ich werde dieses Restaurant nicht empfehlen. — *I will not recommend this restaurant.*

Had a look ☐ **Nearly there** ☐ **Nailed it** ☐

Einkaufen / *Shopping*

der Kuli(s) — *ballpoint pen*
der Schmuck — *jewellery*
die Brieftasche(n) — *wallet*
die Tasse(n) — *mug, cup*
das Tischtuch(-tücher) — *table cloth*
die Kekse (pl) — *biscuits*
der Markt (Märkte) — *market*
der Souvenirladen (-läden) — *souvenir shop*
der Andenkenladen (-läden) — *souvenir shop*
das Kaufhaus(-häuser) — *department store*
das Einkaufszentrum (-zentren) — *shopping centre*
Ich suche ein Geschenk. — *I'm looking for a present.*
Welche Größe? — *What size?*
klein / mittel / groß — *small / medium / large*
Welche Farbe mag er? — *Which colour does he like?*
Seine Lieblingsfarbe ist (rot). — *His favourite colour is (red).*

Had a look ☐ **Nearly there** ☐ **Nailed it** ☐

bunt — *multi-coloured*
(grün-weiß) gestreift — *(green and white) striped*
preiswert — *inexpensive*
teuer — *expensive*
altmodisch — *old-fashioned*
beliebt — *popular*
kaputt — *broken*
kurz — *short*
lang — *long*
schmutzig — *dirty*
im Sonderangebot — *on special offer*
… funktioniert nicht — *… doesn't work*
… hat ein Loch — *… has a hole*

Had a look ☐ **Nearly there** ☐ **Nailed it** ☐

Probleme unterwegs / *Problems out and about*

Mir ist schlecht. — *I feel ill.*
Mir ist schwindelig. — *I feel dizzy.*
Mir ist kalt / heiß. — *I feel cold / hot.*
Der Arm tut mir weh. — *My arm hurts.*
Mir geht es (nicht) gut. — *I'm (not) well.*
Ich bin gefallen. — *I fell over.*
Ich habe meine Schlüssel verloren. — *I have lost my keys.*
Ich habe kein Geld. — *I don't have any money.*
Ich möchte einen Handy-Diebstahl melden. — *I'd like to report a mobile phone theft.*
Sie müssen / Du musst … — *You must …*
zum Restaurant gehen — *go to the restaurant*
zum Fundbüro gehen — *go to the lost property office*
zum Geldautomaten gehen — *go to the cash point*
zur Polizeiwache gehen — *go to the police station*
zur Apotheke gehen — *go to the chemist's*
ins Krankenhaus gehen — *go to hospital*

Had a look ☐ **Nearly there** ☐ **Nailed it** ☐

Kapitel 5 Wörter

Extra words I should know for reading and listening activities

Reisen	Travelling
das Boot(e)	boat
die Fähre(n)	ferry
der Reisebus(-busse)	coach
der Bahnsteig(e)	platform
die Haltestelle(n)	stop (bus, tram, etc.)
der Fahrkartenautomat(en)	ticket machine
der Fahrkartenschalter	ticket office
der Hauptbahnhof	main railway station
das Reisebüro(s)	travel agency
der Speisewagen	dining car, restaurant car (on train)
der Wartesaal	waiting room (at station)
das Gepäck	luggage
der Koffer(-)	suitcase
die Reisetasche(n)	travel bag

Had a look ☐ Nearly there ☐ Nailed it ☐

Unterwegs	On the move
die Fahrt(en)	journey
der Flug (Flüge)	flight
die Reise(n)	journey
die Richtung(en)	direction
die Ermäßigung(en)	reduction
der Fahrpreis(e)	fare
die Verspätung	delay
aussteigen*	to get off (bus / train)
einsteigen*	to get in/on
umsteigen*	to change (means of transport)
entwerten	to stamp, to validate (a ticket)

Had a look ☐ Nearly there ☐ Nailed it ☐

In der Stadt	In town
der/die Besucher(in)	visitor
die Sehenswürdigkeit(en)	tourist attraction, sight
die Busrundfahrt(en)	bus tour
die Führung(en)	guided tour
die Rundfahrt(en)	round trip, tour
der Stadtbummel	stroll through town
die Stadtrundfahrt	sightseeing tour of a town / city
die Öffnungszeiten	opening times
der Stadtplan(-pläne)	town plan / map
die Brücke(n)	bridge
die Burg(en)	(fortified) castle
das Denkmal(e)	monument
der Kirchturm(-türme)	church tower, spire
die Kunstgalerie	art gallery
der Bürgersteig	pavement

der Zebrastreifen	zebra crossing
besichtigen	to sightsee, to visit
sehenswert	worth seeing

Had a look ☐ Nearly there ☐ Nailed it ☐

Essen und trinken	Eating and drinking
die Getränkekarte	drinks menu
das Tagesmenü	menu of the day
das Trinkgeld	tip (for waiter/waitress)
die Eisdiele(n)	ice cream parlour
die Selbstbedienung	self-service
der Speisesaal	dining hall, dining room
die Gabel	fork
das Glas (Gläser)	glass
das Kännchen(-)	pot (tea, coffee)
das Messer	knife
die Tasse(n)	cup
der Teelöffel(-)	teaspoon
der Teller(-)	plate
hausgemacht	home-made
fettig	greasy

Had a look ☐ Nearly there ☐ Nailed it ☐

Einkaufen	Shopping
das Geschäft(e)	shop
die Bäckerei	bakery
die Buchhandlung	book shop
die Drogerie	chemist's
das Kaufhaus(-häuser)	department store
die Konditorei	confectioner's
das Lebensmittelgeschäft	grocer's
die Metzgerei	butcher's
die Reinigung	dry cleaner's
das Warenhaus(-häuser)	department store
die Quittung(en)	receipt
die Rolltreppe(n)	escalator
das Schaufenster(-)	shop window
das Sonderangebot(e)	special offer

Had a look ☐ Nearly there ☐ Nailed it ☐

> ★ *Look carefully at small words at the start of verbs which can change their meaning:
>
> einsteigen to get in/on   Ich **steige** in den Bus **ein**.
> aussteigen to get out/off   Er **steigt** aus dem Zug **aus**.
> umsteigen to change (e.g. trains)   Wir **steigen** in Köln **um**.

Kapitel 6 Wörter

Words I should know for speaking and writing activities

Himmelsrichtungen	*Points of the compass*
der Kompass	compass
der Norden	north
der Nordosten	north east
der Osten	east
der Südosten	south east
der Süden	south
der Südwesten	south west
der Westen	west
der Nordwesten	north west
im Norden	in the north
im Osten	in the east
im Süden	in the south
im Westen	in the west
in der Mitte	in the middle

Had a look ☐   Nearly there ☐   Nailed it ☐

Länder und Orte	*Countries and places*
das Reiseziel	travel destination
das Urlaubsziel	holiday destination
im Ausland	abroad
im Inland	at home, inland
Europa	Europe
Bayern	Bavaria
die Nordsee	the North Sea
die Ostsee	the Baltic Sea
Spanien	Spain
Kroatien	Croatia
Italien	Italy
Österreich	Austria
die Türkei	Turkey

Had a look ☐   Nearly there ☐   Nailed it ☐

Ich fahre ...	*I am going ...*
nach Spanien	to Spain
nach Italien	to Italy
in die Türkei	to Turkey
ans Meer	to the sea
an einen See	to a lake
an den Strand	to the beach
an die Küste	to the coast
in den Wald	to a forest
in die Berge	to the mountains

Had a look ☐   Nearly there ☐   Nailed it ☐

Das Wetter	*The weather*
der Frost	frost
das Gewitter	thunderstorm
der Hagel	hail
der Nebel	fog
der Regen	rain
der Schnee	snow
die Sonne	sun
der Wind	wind
die Wolken (pl)	clouds

Had a look ☐   Nearly there ☐   Nailed it ☐

Es ist ...	*It is ...*
frostig	frosty
heiß	hot
kalt	cold
neblig	foggy
sonnig	sunny
windig	windy
wolkig	cloudy
Es ...	*It is ...*
friert	freezing
hagelt	hailing
regnet	raining
schneit	snowing

Had a look ☐   Nearly there ☐   Nailed it ☐

Es gibt ...	*There is / are ...*
Nebel	fog
ein Gewitter	a thunderstorm
Wolken	clouds
Es wird (heiß) sein.	It will be (hot).
Es wird hageln.	It will hail.
Es wird regnen.	It will rain.
Es wird schneien.	It will snow.
Es wird ein Gewitter geben.	There will be a thunderstorm.
Die Temperatur wird (11) Grad sein.	The temperature will be (11) degrees.

Had a look ☐   Nearly there ☐   Nailed it ☐

die Jahreszeit	season
meine Lieblingsjahreszeit	my favourite season
der Frühling	spring
der Sommer	summer
der Herbst	autumn
der Winter	winter
Die Nächte werden kalt.	The nights become / are becoming cold.
Die Tage werden länger.	The days become / are becoming longer.
Die Tage werden kürzer.	The days become / are becoming shorter.
Das Wetter wird besser.	The weather becomes / is becoming better.

Had a look ☐   Nearly there ☐   Nailed it ☐

K 6

Kapitel 6 Wörter

Urlaubsarten — Types of holidays

Ich mache (nicht) gern …	I (don't) like going on a/an…
Abenteuerurlaub	adventure holiday
Aktivurlaub	active holiday
Sightseeingurlaub	sightseeing holiday
Sommerurlaub	summer holiday
Strandurlaub	beach holiday
Urlaub auf Balkonien	staycation / holiday at home
Winterurlaub	winter holiday
Ich gehe (nicht) gern zelten.	I (don't) like going camping.
Ich gehe (nicht) gern …, weil ich …	I (don't) like going … because I …
abenteuerlustig bin	am adventurous
sportlich bin	am sporty
aktiv bin	am active
gern schwimme	like swimming
gern in der Sonne liege	like sunbathing
gern draußen bin	like being outdoors
gern Zeit mit Familie verbringe	enjoy spending time with family
gern Zeit mit Freunden verbringe	enjoy spending time with friends
mich schnell langweile	get bored easily
nichts tun will	don't want to do anything

Had a look ☐ Nearly there ☐ Nailed it ☐

Urlaubsaktivitäten — Holiday activities

während des Urlaubs	during the holiday
außerhalb der Stadt	outside the town
innerhalb der Stadt	inside the town
wegen des Wetters	because of the weather
trotz der Touristen	despite the tourists
eine neue / aufregende Aktivität	a new / exciting activity
Achterbahn fahren	to go on a rollercoaster
Wanderungen machen	to go hiking
Fahrräder mieten	to rent / hire bicycles
eine Raftingtour machen	to go on a rafting trip
eine Canyoningtour machen	to go on a canyoning trip
die Übernachtung	overnight stay
im Zelt übernachten	to spend the night in a tent
in einer Hütte übernachten	to spend the night in a hut / cabin
im Luxushotel übernachten	to spend the night in a luxury hotel
Vollpension	full board
Halbpension	half board
das Zweibettzimmer	twin room

Had a look ☐ Nearly there ☐ Nailed it ☐

In der Stadt — In town

Es gibt …	There is …
eine Autobahn	a motorway
einen Bahnhof	a station
einen Campingplatz	a campsite
ein Eiscafé	an ice cream café
ein Freibad	an open-air pool
ein Fußballstadion	a football stadium
eine Fußgängerzone	a pedestrianised area
eine Grundschule	a primary school
einen Kindergarten	a nursery
eine Schule	a school

Had a look ☐ Nearly there ☐ Nailed it ☐

Es gibt …	There are …
viele Touristen	lots of tourists
viele Geschäfte	lots of shops
viele Sehenswürdigkeiten	lots of sights
gute Restaurants	good restaurants
viele Vorteile	lots of advantages
viele Nachteile	lots of disadvantages
Es gibt …	There is …
keinen Flughafen	no airport
keine Universität	no university
kein Kino	no cinema
Es gibt keine Strände.	There are no beaches.

Had a look ☐ Nearly there ☐ Nailed it ☐

Meine Stadt: Vor- und Nachteile — My town: advantages and disadvantages

Ich wohne …	I live …
auf einem Bauernhof	on a farm
auf dem Land	in the countryside
in einem Dorf	in a village
in einer Kleinstadt	in a small town
in einer Großstadt	in a city
in einer Hauptstadt	in a capital city
in der Nähe von …	near …
Es gibt …	There is …
viel zu tun	a lot to do
viel Lärm	a lot of noise
viel Verkehr	a lot of traffic
Es gibt nicht viele Autos.	There aren't many cars.
Es gibt nicht viel für Jugendliche zu tun.	There's not much for young people to do.
Es gibt keine Buslinie.	There is no bus route.

Had a look ☐ Nearly there ☐ Nailed it ☐

Es gab …	There was …
einen tollen Park	a great park
ein modernes Sportzentrum	a modern sports centre

Kapitel 6 Wörter

Es gab keine großen Diskos.	There were no big discos.
Es wird keine neue Industrie geben.	There will not be any new industry.
Es wird ein Fußballstadion geben.	There will be a football stadium.
Man sollte …	We should …
mehr Busse haben	have more buses
moderne Sportanlagen haben	have modern sports facilities
mehr Aktivitäten für Jugendliche haben	have more activities for young people
Parkplätze am Stadtrand bauen	build car parks on the outskirts of town
die öffentlichen Verkehrsmittel verbessern	improve public transport
mehr Fahrradwege haben	have more cycle paths
Autos in der Innenstadt verbieten	ban cars from the town centre
die Straßen sauber halten	keep the roads clean
Der Vorteil / Nachteil ist …	The advantage / disadvantage is …
Ein großer Vorteil / Nachteil ist …	A big advantage / disadvantage is …
Es gibt viele Vorteile / Nachteile.	There are lots of advantages / disadvantages.

Had a look ☐ **Nearly there** ☐ **Nailed it** ☐

Kapitel 6 Wörter

Extra words I should know for reading and listening activities

Die Natur / Nature
das Festland	mainland
die Insel(n)	island
die Küste	coast
das Meer(e)*	sea
das Mittelmeer	Mediterranean Sea
der See(n)*	lake
die See(n)*	sea
der Wald (Wälder)	wood, forest
die Wiese(n)	meadow
der Himmel	sky
die Landschaft	landscape
der Baum (Bäume)	tree
das Blatt (Blätter)	leaf (on tree or other plant)

Had a look ☐   Nearly there ☐   Nailed it ☐

Meine Gegend / My area
der Badeort(e)**	seaside resort
das Bauernhaus (-häuser)	farm house
das Gebäude(–)	building
der Einwohner(–)	inhabitant
der Hafen (Häfen)	harbour, port
der Stau(s)	traffic jam
der Supermarkt (-märkte)	supermarket
die Umgebung(en)	surrounding area
die Verbindung(en)	(transport) connection
anbieten	to offer
kontrollieren	to control

Had a look ☐   Nearly there ☐   Nailed it ☐

Im Urlaub / On holiday
der Badeanzug	swimsuit
die Badehose	swimming trunks
der Blick(e)	view, glance
die Erinnerung(en)	memory
das Plakat(e)	poster, billboard
das Formular(e)	form
die Pension(en)	bed and breakfast, guesthouse, (small) hotel
der Wohnwagen**	caravan
das Zelt(e)	tent
die Landkarte(n)	map
die Straßenkarte(n)	road map
das Schließfach (-fächer)	locker
der Sicherheitsgurt(e)	safety belt, seat belt
die Überfahrt(en)	crossing (sea)
erleben	to experience
zelten	to camp
seekrank*	seasick

Had a look ☐   Nearly there ☐   Nailed it ☐

Urlaubsaktivitäten / Holiday activities
die Fahrradvermietung	bicycle hire
der Fotoapparat(e)	camera
das Segelboot(e)	sailing boat
der Sonnenbrand	sunburn
die Sonnencreme	suntan lotion
der Strandkorb (-körbe)	wicker beach chair with a hood
der Yogakurs(e)	yoga course
(sich) sonnen	to sunbathe
windsurfen	to windsurf

Had a look ☐   Nearly there ☐   Nailed it ☐

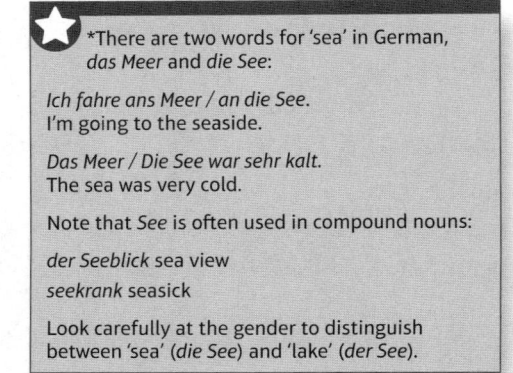

*There are two words for 'sea' in German, *das Meer* and *die See*:

Ich fahre ans Meer / an die See.
I'm going to the seaside.

Das Meer / Die See war sehr kalt.
The sea was very cold.

Note that *See* is often used in compound nouns:

der Seeblick sea view
seekrank seasick

Look carefully at the gender to distinguish between 'sea' (*die See*) and 'lake' (*der See*).

**To work out the meaning of a new word, ask yourself if it is similar to one you already know, and if it contains cognates or near-cognates:

der Wohnwagen → *wohnen* (to live) + *Wagen* (car / van) = literally 'living van', or 'caravan'

der Badeort → *baden* (to swim / to bathe) + *Ort* (place) = literally 'swimming place', or 'seaside resort'

Remember to think beyond the literal translation when working out the correct English meaning.

Words I should know for speaking and writing activities

Berufe / Jobs

der/die Apotheker(in)	chemist
der/die Architekt(in)	architect
der/die Arzt/Ärztin	doctor
der/die Bäcker(in)	baker
der/die Beamte/Beamtin	civil servant
der/die Bibliothekar(in)	librarian
der/die Elektriker(in)	electrician
der/die Fahrer(in)	driver
der/die Feuerwehrmann/-frau	firefighter
der/die Freiwillige	volunteer
der/die Friseur/Friseuse	hairdresser
der/die Informatiker(in)	computer scientist
der/die Journalist(in)	journalist
der/die Kellner(in)	waiter/waitress
der/die Klempner(in)	plumber
der/die Koch/Köchin	cook
der/die Krankenpfleger/Krankenschwester	nurse

Had a look ☐   Nearly there ☐   Nailed it ☐

der/die Lehrer(in)	teacher
der/die Manager(in)	manager
der/die Mechaniker(in)	mechanic
der/die Metzger(in)	butcher
der/die Pilot(in)	pilot
der/die Programmierer(in)	computer programmer
der/die Schauspieler(in)	actor/actress
der/die Sozialarbeiter(in)	social worker
der/die Tierarzt/Tierärztin	vet
der/die Verkäufer(in)	sales assistant
der/die Übersetzer(in)	translator
der/die Zahnarzt/Zahnärztin	dentist

Had a look ☐   Nearly there ☐   Nailed it ☐

Arbeitsorte / Places of work

der Keller(–)	cellar
der Laden (Läden)	shop
die Apotheke(n)	chemist's
die Autowerkstatt (-stätten)	garage
die Bäckerei(en)	bakery
die Bank(en)	bank
die Metzgerei(en)	butcher's
das Büro(s)	office
das Geschäft(e)	shop
der Supermarkt (-märkte)	supermarket
das Krankenhaus (-häuser)	hospital
das Altenheim(e)	elderly care home
das Labor(s)	laboratory
das Reisebüro(s)	travel agency
das Restaurant(s)	restaurant
die Schule(n)	school
das Theater(–)	theatre
die Tierklinik(en)	animal surgery

Had a look ☐   Nearly there ☐   Nailed it ☐

Berufsbilder / Job descriptions

Er/Sie hat ausgezeichnete ... Deutschkenntnisse	He/She has an excellent ... knowledge of German
Sprachkenntnisse	knowledge of languages
Er/Sie ist in (Deutsch) fließend.	He/She is fluent in (German).
Er/Sie kann gut kommunizieren.	He/She can communicate well.
Er/Sie interessiert sich für die technischen Aspekte.	He/She is interested in the technical aspects.
Er/Sie ...	He/She ...
schreibt Reportagen	writes reports
berichtet über aktuelle Themen	reports on current issues
macht Interviews mit Stars	interviews stars
ist zuverlässig	is reliable
ist pünktlich	is punctual

Had a look ☐   Nearly there ☐   Nailed it ☐

Er/Sie hat eine gute Ausbildung.	He/She has a good education.
Ein Hochschulabschluss / Praktikum ist nicht notwendig.	A degree / work experience is not necessary.
Das Gehalt ist niedrig / großzügig.	The salary is low / generous.
Er/Sie arbeitet ...	He/She works ...
bei einer Firma	for a company
in einem Geschäft	in a shop
in einem Altenheim	in an elderly care home
in einem Krankenhaus	in a hospital
in privaten Häusern	in private houses
zuerst	first, firstly
danach	after that
dann	then
schließlich	finally

Had a look ☐   Nearly there ☐   Nailed it ☐

Kapitel 7 Wörter

Berufsprofile — Job profiles

Ich interessiere mich für den Job als …, weil …	I'm interested in the job as … because …
ich (in Mathe) begabt bin	I'm good at / gifted in (maths)
ich (in der Touristik) arbeiten möchte	I would like to work in (tourism)
Seit drei Jahren …	For three years …
bin ich Mitglied im Orchester	I have been a member of an orchestra
bin ich Kapitän der (Handball-)Mannschaft	I have been captain of the (handball) team
gehe ich zum Sportverein	I have been going to a sports club
Ich bekomme gute Noten.	I get good grades.
Meine Noten sind nicht so gut.	My grades are not so good.
Meine Durchschnittsnote ist …	My average grade is …
Ich habe einen Teilzeitjob als (Touristenführer(in)).	I have a part-time job as a (tour guide).
Ich habe einen Ferienjob als …	I have a holiday job as a …
Letzten Sommer habe ich als (Freiwillige(r)) gearbeitet.	Last summer I worked as (a volunteer).

Had a look ☐ **Nearly there** ☐ **Nailed it** ☐

Ich bin …	I am …
kreativ	creative
geduldig	patient
fleißig	hard-working
pünktlich	punctual
Ich konzentriere mich auf den Schulunterricht.	I concentrate on school lessons.
Ich interessiere mich für (das Skifahren).	I am interested in (skiing).
Ich nehme an der (Mathe-Olympiade) teil.	I take part in (the maths olympics).
Ich hoffe auf eine Karriere (in der Touristik).	I am hoping for a career (in tourism).
Ich freue mich auf …	I am looking forward to …

Had a look ☐ **Nearly there** ☐ **Nailed it** ☐

Mein Lebenslauf — My CV

die Schulbildung	school education
der Schulabschluss	school-leaving qualification
der Schulerfolg	school achievement / success
der Hochschulabschluss	degree
die Arbeitserfahrung	work experience
das Hobby(s)	hobby
das Interesse(n)	interest

Had a look ☐ **Nearly there** ☐ **Nailed it** ☐

Traumberufe — Dream jobs

Als Kind wollte ich (Feuerwehrmann / Clown) werden.	As a child, I wanted to become (a firefighter / a clown).
Ich interessiere mich nicht mehr für …	I am no longer interested in …
Ich möchte … arbeiten.	I would like to work …
als (Manager(in))	as a (manager)
im Ausland	abroad
in (den USA)	in (the USA)
freiwillig	voluntarily
bei einer (internationalen) Firma	for an (international) company
beim Zirkus	for a circus
Ich möchte …	I would like …
in einer Hütte in den Alpen wohnen	to live in a hut / cabin in the Alps
nach (Thailand) reisen	to travel to (Thailand)
ein Jahr in (Thailand) verbringen	to spend a year in (Thailand)
eine Lehre machen	to do an apprenticeship
Marketing machen	to do marketing
Ich habe das Abitur (nicht) bestanden.	I passed (did not pass) my A levels.

Had a look ☐ **Nearly there** ☐ **Nailed it** ☐

Sprachen öffnen Türen — Languages open doors

Im Moment lerne ich (Mandarin), um …	At the moment I'm learning (Mandarin) in order to …
Ich möchte (Griechisch) lernen, um …	I would like to learn (Greek) in order to …
mich um einen guten Job zu bewerben	apply for a good job
(in China) zu arbeiten	work (in China)
meine (Deutsch-)Kenntnisse zu verbessern	improve my knowledge of (German)
die Leute besser kennenzulernen	get to know the people better
die Kultur besser kennenzulernen	get to know the culture better
die Sprache besser kennenzulernen	get to know the language better
(die Opern) richtig zu verstehen	understand (the operas) properly
durch das Land zu reisen	travel around the country
mit Leuten in ihrer Muttersprache zu kommunizieren	communicate with people in their native language
nach (Spanien) auszuwandern	emigrate to (Spain)
mich zu amüsieren	have fun
Im Moment lerne ich (Mandarin), weil es … ist.	At the moment I'm learning (Mandarin) because it is …
Pflichtfach	a compulsory subject
nötig / notwendig	necessary, essential
wichtig	important

Had a look ☐ **Nearly there** ☐ **Nailed it** ☐

Kapitel 7 Wörter

Extra words I should know for reading and listening activities

Berufe	*Jobs*
der/die Angestellte	*employee*
der/die Besitzer(in)	*owner*
der/die Chef(in)	*boss*
der/die Kollege/Kollegin	*colleague*
der/die Mitarbeiter(in)	*employee, colleague*
der/die Bauer/Bäuerin*	*farmer*
der/die Bauarbeiter(in)*	*building / construction worker*
der/die Briefträger(in)	*postman/woman*
der/die Fleischer(in)	*butcher*
der/die Fremdsprachenassistent(in)	*foreign language assistant*
der/die Gärtner(in)	*gardener*
die Hausfrau	*house wife*
der Hausmann	*house husband*
der/die Kassierer(in)	*cashier, bank clerk*
der/die LKW-Fahrer(in)	*lorry driver*
der/die Maler(in)	*painter, decorator*
der/die Pfarrer(in)	*parish priest, vicar*
der/die Postbote/Postbotin	*postman/woman*
der/die Rentner(in)	*pensioner*
der/die Tischler(in)	*carpenter*

Had a look ☐ Nearly there ☐ Nailed it ☐

Bei der Arbeit	*At work*
der Bauernhof*	*farm*
die Baustelle*	*building site*
das Büro(s)	*office*
der Friseursalon(s)	*hairdresser's*
im Freien	*outside, in the open air*
der Hausbau	*house building / construction*
der/die Kunde/Kundin	*customer*
die Arbeitszeit	*work hours (pl)*
die Bezahlung(en)	*payment*
der Lohn (Löhne)	*wage*
der Mindestlohn	*minimum wage*
die Stelle(n)	*job*
die Halbtagsarbeit	*part-time / half-day work*
die Schichtarbeit	*shift work*
die Vollzeitarbeit	*full-time work*
gut / schlecht bezahlt	*well / badly paid*
ganztags	*all day*
berufstätig (sein)	*(to be) in work*
anbauen*	*to grow (crops)*
bauen*	*to build*
besitzen	*to own*

Had a look ☐ Nearly there ☐ Nailed it ☐

Studium und Ausbildung	*Studies and training*
der/die Abiturient(in)	*person doing the Abitur*
der Sprachkurs(e)	*language course*
der Sprachunterricht	*language classes*
der Studienplatz (-plätze)	*university place*
die Wirtschaft	*economics (subject)*
der Nebenjob(s)	*part-time job*
das Semester(-)	*term*
das Taschengeld	*pocket money*
theoretisch	*theoretical*
der/die Auszubildende (Azubi)	*apprentice, trainee*
der Ausbildungsplatz (-plätze)	*vacancy / place for a trainee*
der/die Berufsberater(in)	*careers adviser*
die Berufsschule(n)	*vocational training school*
der Rat	*advice*

Had a look ☐ Nearly there ☐ Nailed it ☐

Bewerbungen	*Job applications*
die Bewerbung(en)	*application*
der Brief(e)	*letter*
der Termin(e)	*date, appointment*
das Vorstellungsgespräch(e)	*job interview*
der Wunsch (Wünsche)	*wish*
die Gelegenheit(en)	*opportunity*
der Führerschein	*driving licence*

Had a look ☐ Nearly there ☐ Nailed it ☐

---

*Look out for word families when working out the meaning of words, but remember to use the context of the text to help you too.

Bauen means 'to build' and anbauen means 'to grow' and you have come across several words using the stem bau:

Der Bauer and der Bauarbeiter both look similar, but one means 'farmer' and the other 'builder'.

Der Bauernhof and die Baustelle also look quite similar, but which is a 'farm', and which a 'building site'?

Using the language around the words will help you work out the meaning:

Ich wohne auf einem Bauernhof auf dem Land.
I live on a farm in the countryside.

Here, the verb wohne and the location auf dem Land help you decide that Bauernhof must be a farm rather than a building site.

K7

Kapitel 8 Wörter

Words I should know for speaking and writing activities

Festivals und Events	**Festivals and events**
Mein Lieblingsmusikfestival ist …	My favourite music festival is …
Mein Lieblingsevent ist …	My favourite event is …
die Pariser Modewoche	Paris fashion week
der Eurovision Song Contest	the Eurovision Song Contest
die Fußballweltmeisterschaft	the football World Cup
Mein Lieblingsevent sind …	My favourite event is …
die Filmfestspiele von Cannes	the Cannes Film Festival
die Olympischen Winterspiele	the Winter Olympic Games
die Olympischen Sommerspiele	the Summer Olympic Games
Das Festival / Event findet … statt. in Deutschland / England	The festival / event takes place … in Germany / England
jeden Sommer / Winter	every summer / winter
jedes Jahr	every year
alle vier Jahre	every four years
Ich habe … gesehen / besucht.	I saw / visited …
Das Festival war … sehr interessant / langweilig	The festival was … very interesting / boring
total spannend / toll	totally exciting / great
ziemlich laut	quite loud

Had a look ☐ Nearly there ☐ Nailed it ☐

Die Olympischen Winterspiele	**The Winter Olympics**
Im Jahr (1976) haben die Olympischen Spiele in … stattgefunden.	In (1976) the Olympic Games took place in …
eine Bronzemedaille	a bronze medal
eine Silbermedaille	a silver medal
eine Goldmedaille	a gold medal
Die Athleten haben … Medaillen gewonnen.	The athletes won … medals.
die Baustelle(n)	building / construction works
die Gastgeberstadt (-städte)	host city
die Luftverschmutzung	air pollution
der Stau(s)	traffic jam
die Sprache	language
die Kultur(en)	culture
der Tourist(en)	tourist
der Zeitdruck	time pressure
der Unfall(-fälle)	accident
die Infrastruktur	infrastructure
schmutzig	dirty
unsicher	unsafe
der Einwohner(-)	resident

Had a look ☐ Nearly there ☐ Nailed it ☐

Eine Debatte	**A debate**
Meiner Meinung nach sind die Olympischen Spiele gut / nicht gut, weil …	In my opinion, the Olympic Games are good / not good because …
Ich finde, die Olympischen Spiele sind wichtig / nicht wichtig, weil …	I find the Olympic Games are important / not important because …
Auf der einen Seite …	On the one hand …
Auf der anderen Seite …	On the other hand …
Einerseits …	On the one hand …
Andererseits …	On the other hand …
Ich stimme zu.	I agree.
Ich stimme da nicht zu.	I don't agree.
Vielleicht …, aber …	Perhaps … but …

Had a look ☐ Nearly there ☐ Nailed it ☐

Gesellschaftliche Probleme	**Social problems**
der Alkoholiker	alcoholic (person)
die Zigarette(n)	cigarette
die E-Zigarette(n)	e-cigarette
der Lungenkrebs	lung cancer
trinken	to drink
nehmen	to take
vapen	to vape
aufgeben	to give up
ausprobieren	to try
retten	to save
enthalten	to contain
tödlich	lethal
betrunken	drunk
süchtig	addicted
illegal	illegal
unsozial	antisocial
etwas Neues	something new
nichts Positives	nothing positive
alles Mögliche	everything possible
wenig Spannendes	little that is exciting
viel Negatives	a lot that is negative

Had a look ☐ Nearly there ☐ Nailed it ☐

| Meiner Meinung nach … trinkt man Alkohol, weil das cool ist | In my opinion … people drink alcohol because it's cool |
| raucht man, weil das entspannend ist | people smoke because it's relaxing |

Kapitel 8 Wörter

nimmt man Drogen, weil Freunde es machen	people take drugs because friends do it
Ich finde, …	I find …
Alkohol ist eine Geldverschwendung	alcohol is a waste of money
Rauchen ist teuer	smoking is expensive
Drogen sind schrecklich	drugs are terrible
Man sollte nicht Alkohol trinken, weil das gefährlich ist.	You should not drink alcohol because (drinking alcohol) is dangerous.
Man sollte nicht Zigaretten rauchen, weil das süchtig macht.	You should not smoke cigarettes because (smoking) makes you addicted.
Man sollte nicht Drogen nehmen, weil das ekelhaft / tödlich ist.	You should not take drugs because (taking drugs) is disgusting / lethal.

Had a look ☐ **Nearly there** ☐ **Nailed it** ☐

Die Länder / Countries

Bali	Bali
Brasilien	Brazil
Bulgarien	Bulgaria
Costa Rica	Costa Rica
Deutschland	Germany
Finnland	Finland
Griechenland	Greece
Großbritannien	Great Britain
Italien	Italy
Kanada	Canada
Kroatien	Croatia
Lettland	Latvia
Litauen	Lithuania
die Malediven	the Maldives

Had a look ☐ **Nearly there** ☐ **Nailed it** ☐

Namibia	Namibia
Nepal	Nepal
die Niederlande	the Netherlands
Norwegen	Norway
Portugal	Portugal
Rumänien	Romania
Russland	Russia
Schweden	Sweden
die Schweiz	Switzerland
Südafrika	South Africa
Tschechien	Czech Republic
Ungarn	Hungary
USA	USA
Zypern	Cyprus

Had a look ☐ **Nearly there** ☐ **Nailed it** ☐

Die Armut / Poverty

das Gute	the good thing
das Positive	the positive thing
ungefähr	about, approximately
fast	almost
häufig	often
von Armut bedroht	threatened by poverty
die Ursache(n)	cause
die Arbeitslosigkeit	unemployment
der geringe Lohn (Löhne)	low wage / pay
die Schuld(en)	debt
der Bildungsmangel	lack of education
die Trennung	separation
der Immigrant(en) / die Immigrantin(nen)	immigrant
der/die Obdachlose(n)	homeless person
obdachlos	homeless
arm	poor
das Zuhause(-)	home
die Arbeitsstelle(n)	job
die Arbeitssuche	job search
sich entspannen	to relax
von zu Hause weglaufen	to run away from home
deprimierend	depressing
sicher / unsicher	safe / unsafe

Had a look ☐ **Nearly there** ☐ **Nailed it** ☐

Umwelt macht Schule / Setting environmental standards at school

der Umweltschutz	environmental protection
die Umweltaktion	environmental action
Man sollte …	We should …
eine Solaranlage installieren	install solar panels
den Müll trennen	sort the rubbish
Druckerpatronen / Kopierkartuschen recyceln	recycle printer / copier cartridges
eine Fahrradwoche organisieren	organise a bike week
Energie sparen	save energy
Nistkästen für Vögel bauen	build bird boxes
Obst und Gemüse kompostieren	compost fruit and vegetables
Bienenvölker im Schulgarten halten	keep beehives in the school garden
effektiver recyceln	recycle more effectively
oft	often
leicht	easy
effektiv	effective
schnell	quick
bestimmt	definitely
vielleicht	maybe
nie	never

Had a look ☐ **Nearly there** ☐ **Nailed it** ☐

Kapitel 8 Wörter

Wie werden wir „grüner"?	How do we become 'greener'?
die Dürre	drought
die Luftverschmutzung	air pollution
der saure Regen	acid rain
die Wasserverschmutzung	water pollution
die globale Erwärmung	global warming
die Abholzung	deforestation
das Aussterben von Tierarten	the extinction of animal species
vom Aussterben bedroht	threatened with extinction
die Gletscher schmelzen	the glaciers are melting
Das ist ein großes Problem, weil …	It's a big problem because …
Das größte Problem ist …	The biggest problem is …
Man sollte …	We should …
die Tiere schützen	protect animals
die Wälder nicht zerstören	not destroy forests
mehr Bäume pflanzen	plant more trees
weniger Bäume fällen	cut down fewer trees
weniger abholzen	deforest less

Had a look ☐ **Nearly there** ☐ **Nailed it** ☐

K 8

Kampagnen und gute Zwecke	Campaigns and good causes
Ich will …	I want to …
mit blinden Kindern arbeiten	work with blind children
in einer Schule unterrichten	teach in a school
bei einer Schutzorganisation arbeiten	work for a protection organisation
bei einer Umweltschutzorganisation arbeiten	work for an environmental protection organisation
bei einer Hilfsorganisation arbeiten	work for an aid organisation
Fußball mit armen Kindern spielen	play football with poor children
freiwillig arbeiten	work as a volunteer
der Natur helfen	help nature
der Umwelt helfen	help the environment
Kindern helfen	help children
armen Menschen helfen	help poor people
ein Projekt im Ausland machen	do a project abroad
Straßenkinder	street children
die Partnerschule	partner school

Had a look ☐ **Nearly there** ☐ **Nailed it** ☐

Kapitel 8 Wörter

Extra words I should know for reading and listening activities

Festivals und Events — *Festivals and events*
die Ausstellung(en) — *exhibition*
die Diskussion(en) — *discussion*
der Informationskiosk(e) — *information desk*
das Jugendorchester(–) — *youth orchestra*
der/die Komponist(in) — *composer*
die Kapazität — *capacity (venue)*
der Marathon(s) — *marathon*
die Modenschau(en) — *fashion show*
der Vortag(-träge) — *lecture*

Had a look ☐   Nearly there ☐   Nailed it ☐

Gesellschaftliche Probleme — *Social problems*
das Bewusstsein — *consciousness*
der/die Drogenhändler(in) — *drug dealer*
der/die Drogensüchtige — *drug addict*
die Spraydose(n) — *aerosol*
die Spritze(n) — *syringe, injection*
die Sucht — *addiction*
abhängig sein von — *to be dependent on*
bewusstlos — *unconscious*
schädlich — *harmful*
in der Öffentlichkeit — *in public*
aufhören — *to stop*
enthalten — *to contain*
spritzen — *to inject*

Had a look ☐   Nearly there ☐   Nailed it ☐

Die Armut — *Poverty*
der/die Bettler(in) — *beggar*
der/die Einwanderer/Einwanderin — *immigrant*
der Flüchtling(e) — *refugee*
die Gewalt — *violence*
die Gleichheit — *equality*
das Heim(e) — *home, care home*
der Schlafplatz(-plätze) — *place to sleep*
der Schutz — *protection, shelter*
die Sozialhilfe — *income support*
die Sozialwohnung(en) — *council flat*
die Suppenküche — *soup kitchen*
keinen festen Wohnsitz haben — *to have no fixed abode*
von Armut bedroht — *threatened by poverty*
gewalttätig — *violent*

Had a look ☐   Nearly there ☐   Nailed it ☐

Umweltprobleme — *Environmental problems*
der Abfall (Abfälle) — *rubbish, waste*
der Abfalleimer(–) — *rubbish bin, litter bin*
das Abgas(e) — *exhaust fumes*
das Altpapier — *waste paper*
der Gebrauch — *usage*
die Mülltonne(n) — *dustbin*
die Kohle — *coal*
das Kraftwerk* — *power station*
das Ozonloch — *hole in the ozone layer*
die Ozonschicht — *ozone layer*
der saure Regen — *acid rain*
der Sauerstoff — *oxygen*
der Schaden — *damage*
der Treibhauseffekt — *greenhouse effect*
der Verbrauch — *consumption*
verschmutzen — *to pollute*
zerstören — *to destroy*
umweltfeindlich — *environmentally unfriendly*

Had a look ☐   Nearly there ☐   Nailed it ☐

Wie werden wir „grüner"? — *How do we become 'greener'?*
der Biomüll — *organic waste*
die alternative Energiequelle — *alternative source of energy*
das Gerät(e) — *machine, appliance*
das Licht(er) — *light*
die Luft — *air*
die Regierung(en) — *government*
der/die Umweltsprecher(in) — *environmental representative*
die Verpackung — *packaging*
die Wasserkraft — *hydroelectric power*
atmen — *to breathe*
ausschalten — *to turn off (light, power)*
biologisch (Bio–) — *biological, organic*
bleifrei — *lead-free*

Had a look ☐   Nearly there ☐   Nailed it ☐

K8

41

Kapitel 8 Wörter

Kampagnen und gute Zwecke	*Campaigns and good causes*
die Gesellschaft	*society*
die Krankheit(en)	*illness*
das Menschenrecht(e)	*human right*
das Tierheim(e)	*animal shelter*
die Wohltätigkeits-organisation(en)	*charity (organisation)*
das Wohltätigkeits-konzert(e)	*charity concert*
die Wohltätigkeits-veranstaltung(en)	*charity event*
lohnenswert	*worthwhile*
überbevölkert	*overpopulated*
spenden	*to donate*

Had a look ☐ **Nearly there** ☐ **Nailed it** ☐

⭐ *German words don't always translate directly into English. Sometimes you will need to take the sense of a German word and think a bit more broadly to come up with the correct English translation:*

das Kraftwerk → *Kraft* (power) + *Werk* (works) = 'power station' rather than 'power works'

ISBN 978-1-292-17254-5